Anne Frank on the Postwar Dutch Stage

This book is a case study into the affective history of Holocaust drama offering a new perspective on the impact of *The Diary of Anne Frank*, the pivotal 1950s play that was a turning point in Holocaust consciousness.

Despite its overwhelming success, criticism of the Broadway makeover has been harsh, suggesting that the alleged Americanization would not do justice to the violence of the Holocaust or Anne Frank's budding Jewishness. This study revisits these issues by focusing on the play's European appropriation delving into the emotional intensity with which the play was produced and received. The core of the exploration is a history of the Dutch staging in ethnographic detail, based on unique archival material such as correspondence with Otto Frank, prompt books, original tapes, blueprints of the set and oral history.

This microhistory of the first Dutch performance of the theatrical adaptation of Anne Frank's diary examines the staging in the context of the postwar hesitant development of publicly voiced Holocaust consciousness. Influenced by memory studies and affect theory, the emphasis is on the emotional impact of the drama on both the members of the cast and the audience and will be of great interest to students and scholars in theater and performance studies, memory studies, cultural history, Jewish studies, Holocaust studies and contemporary European history.

Remco Ensel is Assistant Professor in the Department of History, Art History and Classics at Radboud University, the Netherlands.

Routledge Advances in Theatre & Performance Studies

This series is our home for cutting-edge, upper-level scholarly studies and edited collections. Considering theatre and performance alongside topics such as religion, politics, gender, race, ecology, and the avant-garde, titles are characterized by dynamic interventions into established subjects and innovative studies on emerging topics.

Włodzimierz Staniewski and the Phenomenon of "Gardzienice"
S. E. Gontarski, Tomasz Wiśniewski and Katarzyna Kręglewska

Anne Frank on the Postwar Dutch Stage
Performance, Memory, Affect
Remco Ensel

Female Aerialists in the 1920s and early 1930s
Femininity, Celebrity & Glamour
Kate Holmes

D'Oyly Carte
The Decline and Fall of an Opera Company
Paul Seeley

Performing Resilience for Systemic Pain
Meghan Moe Beitiks

Performance of Absence in Theatre, Performance and Visual Art
Sylwia Dobkowska

For more information about this series, please visit: www.routledge.com/Routledge-Advances-in-Theatre – Performance-Studies/book-series/RATPS

Anne Frank on the Postwar Dutch Stage

Performance, Memory, Affect

Remco Ensel

LONDON AND NEW YORK

First published 2022
by Routledge
2 Park Square, Milton Park, Abingdon, Oxon OX14 4RN

and by Routledge
605 Third Avenue, New York, NY 10158

Routledge is an imprint of the Taylor & Francis Group, an informa business

British Library Cataloguing-in-Publication Data
A catalogue record for this book is available from the British Library

Library of Congress Cataloging-in-Publication Data
A catalog record for this book has been requested

ISBN: 978-1-032-03429-4 (hbk)
ISBN: 978-1-032-03430-0 (pbk)
ISBN: 978-1-032-03432-4 (ebk)

DOI: 10.4324/9781032034324

Typeset in Times New Roman
by Apex CoVantage, LLC

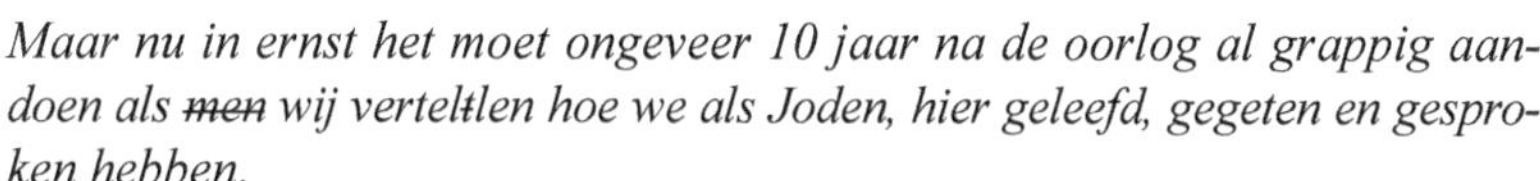

Maar nu in ernst het moet ongeveer 10 jaar na de oorlog al grappig aandoen als ~~men~~ wij vertel~~t~~len hoe we als Joden, hier geleefd, gegeten en gesproken hebben.

But seriously now, ten years after the war it must seem quite funny if ~~it were told~~ we were to tell how we lived here as Jews, what we ate and what we were talking about.

Anne Frank, Diary March 29, 1944 (B)

Contents

Figures

Figure 1 Martine Crefcoeur (1935–2020). The portrait is from 1962 when *The Diary of Anne Frank* was televised (Nationaal Archief/Collectie Spaarnestad/C. Ferguson)

Preface

Research for this monograph started in the archives at a time of a global health crisis. The Gelders Archief (GA), the Allard Pierson Library that holds the theater collection of the University of Amsterdam (UvA), the Maria Austria Institute (MAI) and the Literature Museum (LM) accommodated research in the best possible way, by either sending documents or allowing consultation under special conditions. Their records are indicated by the aforementioned abbreviations. Theatergroep Oostpool granted access to the restricted part of the archive of the ensemble Theater (GA). The audiovisual archive Beeld en Geluid (B&G) digitized a fragment of a TV recording, Maarten Eilander did the same for three original audio reels. The Anne Frank Trust gave permission to include a page from the diary and the NIOD Institute for War, Holocaust and Genocide Studies provided the actual scan.

I am much obliged to the following correspondents for just the right answers to my queries: Gertjan Broek (Anne Frank Stichting), Martien Frijns, Sis Hoek, Johan Kuiper (Harry Mulisch Huis), Sandra Langereis, Sarah A. Lichtman, Dirkje Mulder-Boers, Boudewijn Smits and Abram de Swaan. I thank stage director Johan Doesburg for an insightful interview. Jan Hein Furnée once again proved to be an enthusiastic and astute reader.

Looking for further traces of the play, research took on a whole new affective dimension, especially at a time of renewed physical contacts after the first lockdown. I am immensely grateful to Felix Guttmann for letting me inspect his father's personal archive (KG), stage director Karl Guttmann. Early on, Felix showed me two carton boxes with the invitation to peruse them at my own discretion. The same welcome reception was given to me by Edwin de Vries, son of Robert de Vries, managing director of the ensemble that staged the play. The encounters with two actors from the original cast were moving: Jules Croiset was cast as Peter at 19, Anne-Marie Heyligers played Margot at 25. Martine Crefcoeur (1935–2020) took on the role of Anne Frank when she was still at drama school. Ms Crefcoeur was one of the first victims of COVID-19 in the Netherlands and I heartily dedicate this monograph to her memory.

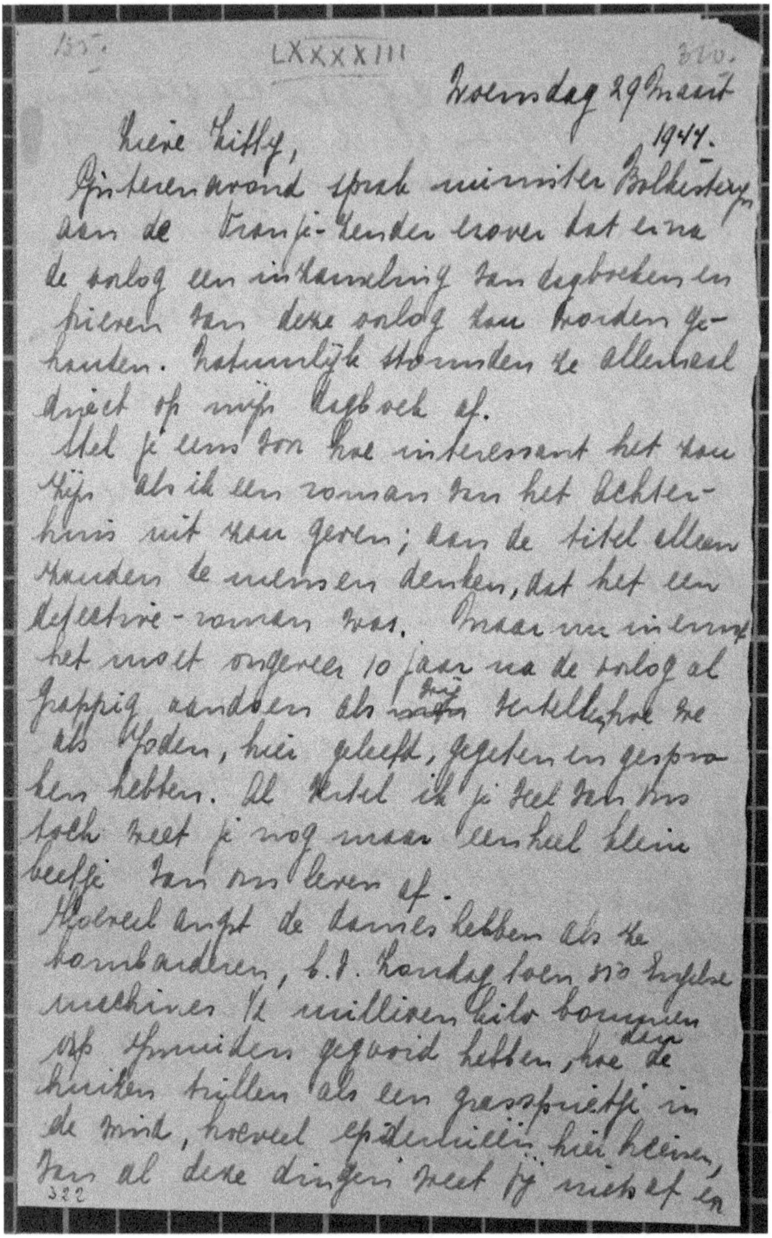

LXXXIII

Woensdag 29 Maart 1944.

Lieve Kitty,

Gisterenavond sprak minister Bolkestein aan de Oranje-Zender erover dat er na de oorlog een inzameling van dagboeken en brieven van deze oorlog zou worden gehouden. Natuurlijk stormden ze allemaal direct op mijn dagboek af.

Stel je eens voor hoe interessant het zou zijn als ik een roman van het Achterhuis uit zou geven; aan de titel alleen zouden de mensen denken, dat het een detective-roman was. Maar nu in ernst, het moet ongeveer 10 jaar na de oorlog al grappig aandoen als wij vertellen hoe we als Joden, hier geleefd, gegeten en gesproken hebben. Al vertel ik je veel van ons, toch weet je nog maar een heel klein beetje van ons leven af.

Hoeveel angst de dames hebben als ze bombarderen, b.v. Zondag toen 350 Engelse machines ½ millioen kilo bommen op IJmuiden gegooid hebben, hoe de huizen trillen als een grassprietje in de wind, hoeveel epidemieën hier heersen, van al deze dingen weet jij niets af en

Figure 2 '[I]t must seem quite funny if we were to tell how we lived here as Jews.' A page from the diary entry of March 29, 1944, in the edited version (facsimile, NIOD Institute for War, Holocaust and Genocide Studies)

Introduction

Specters of Anne Frank

Inspired by a call on Radio Oranje, Anne Frank came up with a plan to edit the diary in which she had recorded her life in hiding for almost two years, meanwhile pondering the reception by a future audience: 'But seriously now, ten years after the war it must seem quite funny if we were to tell how we lived here as Jews, what we ate and what we were talking about.'[1] It was a good hunch, but she might have misjudged the prevailing feelings ten years later. Funny wasn't what came to mind when a stage adaptation of her diary premiered. Some European shows were particularly awkward as people abstained from applause or suppressed their pleasure; many left the theater dejected. Karl Guttmann called the performances he directed a shiva, a Jewish mourning ceremony, others were reminded of a requiem. 'We're carving a gravestone,' one critic realized when it was announced on the Frankfurt stage that Anne Frank was born in that same city on June 12, 1929.[2]

The discrepancy between Anne's projections and the outcome ten years later is somewhat deceptive. Reading through the diary entry for that day – March 29, 1944 – it becomes clear she was aiming for more than just an entertaining memoir. Anne Frank wished to convey the experiences and feelings of the *achterhuizers* or *annexants*, as she called her co-residents of the secret annex, realizing she would fall short and her fictitious correspondent Kitty would 'still know very little': concerning the fear during the air raids, the hunger, the dreams about postwar life, the intense pressure and the gnawing uncertainty about a swift and satisfying end to the war. How to put those feelings into words? The real contrast lay elsewhere, in the outside world where a genocide was unfolding, one that the walls of 'Fort Annex' ultimately failed to hold back.[3]

Anne Frank continues to play a key role in global dialogues about mass violence well beyond the ten years she envisioned, first as the author of her imposing diary and second as a specter – at one time summoned, at other times haunting the present unsolicited. Ten years ago, the volume *Anne*

DOI: 10.4324/9781032034324-1

Frank Unbound took stock of the diary's *Nachleben* nearly 70 years after the publication, showcasing a wide variety of creative expressions that helped propagate the diary through time. In her contribution, theater historian Edna Nahshon regarded the first stage adaptation as one of the most influential of these makeovers. The production was a 'watershed event' for being 'the first time that the mainstream American theater presented a play whose plot focused on the Holocaust.'[4] Arguably, the gravity of the event was felt even more in Europe. At a time when people's habitus was to keep war emotions at bay, the play was accompanied by a remarkable public outburst of emotions. In his report of the Berlin production, *The Observer*'s critic Kenneth Tynan spoke of 'the most dramatic emotional experience the theatre has ever given me.' It 'had little to do with art, because the play was not a great one.' Yet 'it invaded the privacy of the whole audience. I tried hard to stay detached but the general catharsis engulfed me.'[5] The critic took this for a particular European sentiment. Attending the play in New York, 'it smacked of exploitation,' whereas here, at the heart of the catastrophe, it seemed more urgent. 'I can only record an emotion that I felt, would not have missed and pray to never feel again.' Tynan's article was an acute self-analysis, confirming both the affective intensity of the performance and its transgressive enjoyment. It very much seems Holocaust scholar Lawrence Langer's argument that an audience 'in 1955, only a decade after the event, would find little to threaten their psychological or emotional security,' seems to be valid only if European productions were excluded.[6]

This monograph seeks to chart the play's first staging in the Netherlands where it aroused a similar frenzy as in Germany but because of the country's occupied status with a more ambiguous resonance. While the play seemed to endorse the Dutch self-image of heroes and victims, the production also provided disturbing food for thought.

What happens when a harrowing autobiographical document written in war-torn Netherlands returns home after being subjected to an overseas Broadway adaptation? With this question in mind, I began my research in the ensemble's archives and correspondence and the unregistered director's archive – with the crucial supplement featuring interviews from two members of the original cast. Taking Nahshon's qualification of the play as an event seriously, I tried to look beyond the script and delve into the idiosyncrasies of the Dutch production: the effect of the US buzz, the acquisition of the rights, the play's setup – from diary to book production, from script to opening night – as well as the play's short-term and lasting affective bearing on cast, critics and audiences. *Anne Frank on the Postwar Dutch Stage* is my account of how a theater company led by two Holocaust survivors took up a Broadway play and, in an uphill battle, conjured up a troubling past that, through subsequent performative acts, contributed to widening circles of solidarity and empathetic understanding.

Performance

The Diary of Anne Frank premiered at the Cort theater in New York on October 5, 1955. The play turned Anne's poignant diary into an inspiring moral tale. Here was a girl who, in the darkest hour of modern European history, has been deprived of everything a 13-year-old is entitled to – security, privacy, movement, inspiring encounters and innocence – and still finds the strength to respond to the world with hope, humor and self-reflection. From that mighty diary full of memorable contemplations and everyday concerns, the dramatists Frances Goodrich and Alfred Hackett, hereinafter referred to as the Hacketts, isolated the aphorism that became the play's vignette: 'In spite of everything I still believe that people are really good at heart.' The aphorism provided a key to align the diary with further mnemonic activities and trace the recent past of genocidal persecution.

The play's impact stretched far and wide. Sales skyrocketed, first with the triumph of the dramatization and then with the feature film based on the play. The fact that the script won the Pulitzer Prize without meeting the requirement that its plot is situated in America, can in retrospect be seen as a validation of the universalization that Anne's father and sole survivor Otto Frank was aiming for. Anne's Broadway and Hollywood makeovers conquered the hearts of many and the chronicle of the eight unfortunate residents of the annex and their benevolent helpers became one of the most persuasive accounts of the Holocaust – long before the latter term was widely used.

When the first biography appeared in the wake of the European staging, the play was already gaining the upper hand over Anne's legacy. A reader's disappointment was likely, Anne's biographer meditated, because his protagonist came across 'as frailer and less dominant' than the Anne Frank 'who crosses the stage night after night somewhere in the world, entangled in life . . . wearing a different face in every theater.'[7] Even the informants who knew Anne up close felt compelled to respond to her image on stage. Personal encounters, affective memories and reading experiences were mediated by the force of the global staging.

The play is included in the Holocaust Theatre Catalog and the literature, scholarly and otherwise, is comprehensive and enduring.[8] These latter features are due in part to the release of the diary's critical edition of 1986 and the subsequent script update. Overall, the reception has been dismissive. Like no other, the play was lambasted in Gene A. Plunka's tour d'horizon

Holocaust Drama: The Theater of Atrocity.[9] The diary's real objective would have been undermined for commercial and political motives, the playscript contains a Communist message and degenerates into a family drama. 'No one in the play dies or is tortured,' the Nazis are nowhere to be seen and the play doesn't 'do justice to the Holocaust experience.' In a notorious op-ed, American writer Cynthia Ozick took this a step further by repudiating the diary's status as Holocaust document because 'the crimes we have come to call the Holocaust were enacted' outside of the secret annex.[10] Perceived inconsistencies between diary and stage adaptation provoked more critical responses. There was praise for the skillful professionalism of a well-made play, but various critics spurned the fictional additions and the depiction of Anne as a frisky ingenue. The play would not be faithful to the diary, could not count as the main representation of the Shoah that it quickly became and operated primarily to acquit Gentiles – who were after all essentially 'good at heart.' Many were quick to reject the play for its Broadway melodrama.[11]

Now one could argue that the diary contains an unparalleled family drama and that there are indeed no Nazis to be found in it. As it can be maintained that the torturous force exerted on Anne Frank's subjugated body was both subtle and pervasive; that Anne was persecuted for more than two years; that the diary is filled with the terrifying imagination of mass murder; and that according to Ozick's reasoning, people who survived persecution by going into hiding did not experience 'the Holocaust.' But such fidelity criticism is not the course of this monograph. I am less occupied with the script's fundamental gist or timeless aesthetics and more with its performative effects.

To start with the first. The diary is not open to just one interpretation and neither is the script. It would indeed have been exciting if there were multiple scripts. But alas. Only one adaptation was available for over 40 years. In the Netherlands, unlike in Germany, only one ensemble was given the right to produce that one play. These are the effects of distinctive theatrical fields that help define both cast and audience experiences.

I don't see the script as a flawed copy of the diary nor as the end point of a theater production. Research began from the proposition that a script carries its own history and future. The script existed thanks to the diary as a remain from the past and was enriched as soon as it was performed to audiences and thus became accessible to versatile interpretations. This is what made the performances as produced and experienced in a collective effort so deeply humane. What the aforementioned Frankfurt critic may not have known was that Karl Guttmann had changed the phrase from 'born in Germany' to 'born in Frankfurt' to accommodate the setting.[12] It was just the right dramatic *affect* to impress a local audience.

Second, Ozick and Plunka's statements can be seen as being driven not only by conventional fidelity criticism but also by an understanding that the script must faithfully represent an historical past. That's a legitimate provision, but it's not exactly the one followed here. For me, the central question is not what the play was supposed to represent but what it achieved. In this regard, Vivian M. Patraka spoke of a Holocaust performative, while Ernst van Alphen introduced the notion of a Holocaust effect.[13] Both did so to distinguish their approach from one that understands art as a symbolic representation (of the past). Stressing the performative (effects) de-emphasizes the meaning of the script to draw attention to what the play generated.

Both the Shoah and Jewishness came to be understood in the light of the figure of Anne Frank as an inspirational author and a meaningful trace. Anne Frank became the 'Holocaust Jew,' as literary scholar James E. Young argued, 'a two-sided metonymy for both Jewishness and Holocaust.'[14] At a time when terms and tropes were still in full swing, the play helped solidify traces and signs to manifest the genocidal past.

It is significant that, although the word 'Holocaust' was barely in circulation, Plunka speaks of Holocaust drama – adding that the play was one of the first in line. The play was an original in a collection but at the same time did not live up to the criteria. Just as the label of Holocaust drama excludes plays that could very well operate as vehicles of memorization, but would not fit into such a future thematic collection. There is, in other words, an understanding of an archive that simultaneously collects and determines what can be considered as a correct representation.[15]

The argument here is that we need to re-problematize the relationship between diary and script and between both texts and an absent historical past. These are relationships in which reiteration occurs by arbitrary citation, acknowledging some traces and ignoring others.[16] And, let's not forget, which was done from a perspective – bottom-up, from the margin and from inside – that went against a long history of memorizing war and violence.[17]

These are delicate issues. The sense that neither theater nor other artistic accomplishments were able to convey the enormity of the Shoah has been debated at least since Theodor Adorno's dictum about the impossibility of writing poetry after Auschwitz – the phrase that itself became an aphorism and just so put 'Auschwitz' on the map. A crisis of signification can indeed be identified surrounding the staging of the Anne Frank play. Aside from moral objections, there was a feeling that affective memories could not be adequately expressed, let alone converted into cultural memory.[18]

By examining the many versatile cast, critic and audience engagements, this monograph aims to show how the actual production was one performative, albeit a highly influential one, amid less conspicuous interconnected acts: other plays, audience behavior, speeches and commemorative rituals.

Holocaust consciousness, understood as empathy and solidarity, surfaced in such dialogic commemorative acts.

Memory

When in May 1940, the Netherlands was invaded by neighboring Germany, 140,000 Dutch civilians and refugees were put in immediate danger. The Jewish population was highly varied in terms of their religious commitment, social background and ancestral identity. The Frank family belonged to the first influx of German refugees after the Nazi seizure of power. The November pogroms of 1938 led to a new influx of refugees for which a refugee camp was set up near Westerbork, in the north of the country. In the summer of 1942, when Anne Frank turned 13, this camp was converted into the main hub for deportations to the concentration camps abroad. About 29,000 people went into hiding, including the Frank family, together with the Van Pels family – father, mother, son – and dentist Fritz Pfeffer. A few weeks earlier, Anne had begun to write in her new diary and she would continue to do so for the next 26 months. In the last few months, Anne started editing the entries, probably with a view to a postwar publication. After her death, Otto Frank put together a book publication. French, German and English translations soon followed.

After the five-year occupation, it turned out that three-quarters of the Jewish population had been murdered. Few feelings of grief and resentment reached the public sphere and there was little recognition of the specific fate befell Jewish citizens. On the contrary, survivors who were often left empty-handed were charged for arrears of rent and taxes. Antisemitism flared up.[19]

This brief history set the stage for the production of the play during 1954–1958, a moment in time when the effects of war and destruction were still pervasive in the visible physical remains of the occupation, the loss of loved ones and the isolation of survivors, but which was also a time of looking ahead and desiring closure, eyes set on the future. A culture of remembrance had been established in the public sphere – largely avoiding the Shoah. Jewish life was in ruins, but recovery had begun here too.

In the Netherlands, Anne Frank was still very much part of a *milieu de mémoire* and less the global *lieu de mémoire* of today. Various theatergoers and readers of the diary had known her or her family personally. The play hinted at events still fresh in the minds of spectators. For the cast, the play's theme wasn't some far-off affair either. This monograph seeks to zoom in on this pivotal moment in the transfer from individual, social to cultural memory.

The play as a mnemonic act intervened in the public sphere by addressing feelings of loss and curbed memories. It is with this argument in mind that in the chapters to follow, the production of the play is approached in terms of absence-and-presence. Memory is by definition based on identifying traces of a non-presence. Historian Aleida Assmann in her exploration of the metaphors of memory makes a distinction here between storage – of these traces – and an active retrieval.[20] Shards from the past, such as the diary, were excavated and deployed to manifest a past, while involuntary memories forced themselves as intrusive specters.[21] As an event, *The Diary of Anne Frank* conjured up Anne's story as a flash from the past, as described by Walter Benjamin – in his *On the Concept of History* (1939) – in trying to grasp the novelty of the event, while simultaneously recognizing the recurrence of past catastrophes.[22] I connect Benjamin's view on the articulation of atrocities with the way in which Michael Rothberg sees Shoah memorization as a dialogic act of citing and cross-referencing through time and space.[23]

Affect

The impact of the play is better understood when viewed in conjunction with parallel acts of memorization. It is through the reiterative circulation of 'Anne Frank' as a sign that an affective transfer was possible. Putting the spotlight on the dramatization of the diary then amounts to a study in the production and reproduction of affect. Anne Frank and the diary were aligned with a family of objects of affect, citing 'war,' 'persecution,' hiding, the secret annex and the camps where Anne was incarcerated – a process of figures, sites and citations sliding over from one to the other. It is through such a circular process – as proposed by Sara Ahmed – that subjective bodies surfaced, allowing for an empathic understanding between humans in time and space.[24]

The conceptual history of empathy, an English translation of the German *Einfühlung*, is capricious. At first it referred to an intimate, almost bodily connection with artifacts, 'transferring' one's feelings 'into the forms and shapes of objects.' In the course of the twentieth century, the concept's meaning changed to take on the experiences of other persons. Empathy only became part of the everyday vocabulary since the 1950s. Benjamin, in his French translation of *On the Concept of History*, spoke of *identification affective* to refer to the German *Einfühlung* as the habit of putting yourself in someone else's shoes, through time and space. Such an affective transfer, as historian Suzan Lanzoni argues, could come about in the theater – paradoxically best known for the fierce opponent of empathic theater, Bertolt Brecht.[25] Empathy became something to be enacted, in the theater it 'mediated a variety of effects between audience and performer, author and reader, and writer and character.'[26]

All these much-discussed themes are addressed here through the lens of the activities of one ensemble whose members were intimately involved in the persecutions. Robert ('Rob') de Vries experienced the Shoah in the Netherlands as a resistance fighter and prisoner, Karl Guttmann fled from occupied Poland through Russia to Palestine from where he arrived in the Netherlands in the 1950s. Both had been persecuted in the war as Jews, but they carried a different life history and sense of Jewishness. The staging of the play was at a crossroads of different Jewish histories and experiences that are rarely mentioned in connection with the play, but which crop up when focusing on the Dutch production.

Actor and ensemble manager Rob de Vries immediately saw the potential of the play, and when the dramatists visited Amsterdam, he took the opportunity to inquire about an option on the play. However, it would take quite a bit of effort to achieve his goal, partly because Otto Frank got cold feet after some critical survivor responses. Anticipating potential concerns, De Vries instructed Karl Guttmann to co-produce a play that 'would do the Jews good.'[27]

Even a box office hit couldn't convince everyone of the need for a dramatization. Different sentiments ran through the ensemble. Some of the cast members were up to their necks in the war. One young actress questioned the ethics of the venture, a young actor discovered his Jewishness much later, with dire consequences. The staging of the play was an interventionist mnemonic act that anticipated widespread public debate. It touched on feelings that had been kept private, tucked away, or not fully articulated. Perhaps it was the least obvious way to present the Shoah in the public domain – not being a Warsaw Monument or Paul Celan poem – but it was no less dramatic.

Notes

1 Diary references follow the distinction that was introduced in the critical edition: Harry Paape, Gerrold van der Stroom and David Barnouw, eds., *De dagboeken van Anne Frank* (The Hague and Amsterdam, 1986). (A) Anne's original entries, (B) Anne's revision, (C) the book edition.
2 *NIW*, May 22, 1992; *Frankfurter Rundschau*, January 21, 1957.
3 Frank, June 13, 1944 (C).
4 Edna Nahshon, 'Anne Frank from page to stage,' in *Anne Frank unbound: Media, imagination, memory*, eds. Barbara Kirshenblatt-Gimblett and Jeffrey Shandler (Bloomington, 2012), 59–92.
5 Kenneth Tynan, 'Berlin postscript,' *The Observer*, October 7, 1956.
6 Lawrence L. Langer, 'The Americanization of the Holocaust,' in *A scholarly look at The Diary of Anne Frank*, ed. Harold Bloom (Philadelphia, 1999), 15–34.
7 Ernst Schnabel, *Anne Frank: A portrait in courage* (New York, 1958), 16.
8 The Holocaust Theatre Catalog, https://htc.miami.edu/.

9 Gene A. Plunka, *Holocaust drama: The theater of atrocity* (Cambridge, 2009), 101–113.
10 Cynthia Ozick, 'Who owns Anne Frank?,' *The New Yorker*, September 28, 1997.
11 For key texts, see: *Anne Frank unbound*; *A scholarly look at The Diary of Anne Frank*; Hyman A. Enzer and Sandra Solataroff-Enzer, eds., *Anne Frank: Reflections on her life and legacy* (Urbana and Chicago, 2000); Louise Hawker, ed., *Genocide in Anne Frank's the diary of a young girl* (Detroit, 2012).
12 KG: Prompt book for Frankfurt.
13 Vivian M. Petraka, *Spectacular suffering: Theatre, fascism, and the Holocaust* (Bloomington, 1999); Ernst van Alphen, *Caught by history: Holocaust effects in contemporary art, literature, and theory* (Stanford, 1997).
14 James E. Young, *Writing and rewriting the Holocaust: Narrative and the consequences of interpretation* (Bloomington, 1988), 109–113.
15 On the archive, see: Jacques Derrida, 'Archive fever: A Freudian impression,' *Diacritics* 25, 2 (1995): 9–63; Aleida Assmann, *Cultural memory and Western civilization: Functions, media, archives* (Cambridge, 2011), 327–332.
16 For deconstruction, representation, and theater, see Jacques Derrida, 'The theater of cruelty and the closure of representation,' in *Writing and difference* (London and New York, 2001), 292–316.
17 On war narratives, see: Nanci Adler, Remco Ensel and Michael Wintle, eds., *Narratives of war: Remembering and chronicling battle in twentieth-century Europe* (London, 2019).
18 Assmann, *Cultural memory and Western civilization*, 246–255.
19 Dienke Hondius, *Return: Holocaust survivors and anti-semitism* (Westport, 2003).
20 Assmann, *Cultural memory and Western civilization*, 140–145.
21 Jacques Derrida, *Spectres of Marx: The state of the debt, the work of mourning and the new international* (New York, 1993).
22 Walter Benjamin, 'On the concept of history,' in *Fire alarm: Reading Walter Benjamin's "On the concept of history"*, ed. Michael Löwy (London, 2016), 42–46 (thesis VI).
23 Michael Rothberg, *Multidirectional memory: Remembering the Holocaust in the age of decolonization* (Stanford, 2009); see also: Jacques Derrida, *Sjibbolet: Voor Paul Celan* (Nijmegen, 2015), section III.
24 Sara Ahmed, 'Affective economies,' *Social Text* 22, 2 (2004): 117–139; Sara Ahmed, *The cultural politics of emotion* (Edinburgh, 2004).
25 Yet, in fact, Benjamin cites an empathic line from *Die Dreigroschenoper*. Benjamin, 'On the concept of history,' 46–57 (thesis VII).
26 Suzan Lanzoni, *Empathy: A history* (New Haven, 2018), 1–18, 193–201.
27 *NIW*, February 24, 1984.

Figure 3 *Trojan Women* by Euripides in Emmen (1955), a small town near Westerbork. The performance was by seniors of the Emmen Lyceum and directed by Karl Guttmann (school jubilee book; collection Sis Hoek)

1 Time out of joint

Theaters of destruction

We saw their children play in our streets. . . . They have vanished but their presence cannot be unseen.

–Jacob Cramer, Provincial Governor

A small town near Westerbork

Emmen is a small town in Drenthe, the least urbanized province of the Netherlands. In this northeastern border area, the earliest inhabitants are said to have lived, thanks to the many surviving prehistoric megaliths, but the area was not included in the Dutch Republic that fought the Eighty Years' War against the rule of Habsburg Spain, the real founding moment of the nation. The swampy territory interspersed with spots of sand and some habitation only became a fully-fledged province in the nineteenth century. Sheep were introduced to enable arable farming on the poor soils, which generated the expansion of large tracts of heathland. The population increased when the extraction of peat as fuel took on great proportions. Poor families were attracted to the labor in the peatlands, usually moving from one field to the next. They had to dig the canals and then cut the peat, the accumulated residue of Ice Age plants, into straight blocks. As the last peatland still in operation, many families settled near Emmen in the twentieth century. Another influx of residents came about through initiatives by charities to transfer the 'socially maladaptive' at a distance from Holland's thriving cities.

This history provided the backdrop for designating Drenthe as a suitable location for a refugee camp after the German and Austrian pogroms of 1938. Situated on a deserted plain, 25 kilometers from Emmen, the camp remained hidden from view of the civilian population. 'Our shoes sink into the mud and mold. May we be so indecent and request for wellies?,' one of the first refugees wrote to his Dutch friend who eventually was incarcerated in the same camp after the German occupation of the Netherlands.[1] By then

DOI: 10.4324/9781032034324-2

the camp had been transformed into a *Durchgangslager* from which more than 100,000 detainees were sent from 1942 to Auschwitz and other sites of annihilation. In that same year, 180 Jewish residents from Emmen had been gathered one evening by the local police and sent to Westerbork. In August 1944, Anne Frank arrived at the camp after being arrested along with her seven fellow residents from the secret annex. After one month, the eight unfortunates were deported to Auschwitz. With the exception of Mr. Frank, they all perished in different camps in Europe.

Even before the war, the population of Emmen had increased in number and the village had grown in size. After the war, local and central elites joined forces to provide for the corresponding infrastructure and urban ambience. Actually, they did a lot more. A civilizing mission was launched to turn Emmen into a splendid showcase of modernist upgrading. In ten years, industry was lured to the region to compensate for the declining peat industry while urban planners reinvented the town plan by designing residential apartments in geometric shapes, schools and a shopping mall situated in a green scenery. Not only did public space have to modernize, peat workers had to become town dwellers, and that transition required a new and modern attitude to life, education and taste. First subsidized culture was brought to the former peat villages to prevent cultural lag, as the expected discrepancy between rapid technological change and slow cultural adaptation was called. Then the families themselves had to move to Emmen and transform into the workers of the town's new textile and synthetic fiber industry.

The transformation of Emmen was spectacular, but similar developments could be witnessed in other parts of the country. In the 1950s, the early years of reconstruction were over. Germany had reestablished itself in Europe and the border with the Netherlands was reopened. The debris had been cleared, the prosecution of Nazis largely halted. After the debacle of the decolonization war in the late 1940s, the Dutch turned their eyes to the future. A modernization offensive, the foundations of which had already been laid before the war, could be accelerated partly, thanks to overseas financial aid. Europe arose in a process of Americanization. How did this forward-looking period of reconstruction and modernization relate to the traumatic past of mass violence?

In the Netherlands, a series of remembrance practices had been set up around the central belief that for five years the country had been the victim of the greatest possible oppression but that, thanks to the perseverance of the people, of which some had taken a particularly heroic stance, the nation could look back with heads held high. Public commemoration took place through a thread of national memorial sites for which a repertory of ritual acts had been developed. The persecution of the Jews had no distinct place in this. There were no public mourning rituals nor did the government recognize separate victim groups except for the heroes of the resistance. There was the occasional flare that sparked controversy, a case dredged up from the past or an ill-formulated statement, but there was no collective language or set of practices. Critical knowledge and sensitivity to the immensity of the mass murder was not simply lacking, but lingered 'subsumed and subliminal.'[2] At best what was later termed Holocaust consciousness was denoted in oblique terms.

It seems that postwar Drenthe, like the country as a whole, with the wave of modernization that flooded the region, sought to leave the past behind as quickly as possible spending no time looking back. 'In the name of progress, much had to be cleaned up and forgotten,' as one study on the surge of modernization put it, creating a screen memory 'cleansed of all sorts of disturbing facts and details.'[3] The best illustration is the way in which camp Westerbork was reused and abandoned. First it was employed to incarcerate those eligible for transitional justice, then to house repatriates from Indonesia. Finally, the site was left to ruin. Other prison camps were more suited to the postwar nationalist narrative of oppression and resistance. Until the 1970s, the authorities made no successful effort to recall the Shoah past. It was not until almost all material remains of the Durchgangslager were erased – and made way for a huge observatory – that locals began to turn the site into a memorial.

Still, that is not all that transpired. Postwar dealings with the past were multidirectional, as Michael Rothberg convincingly argued in his groundbreaking study of early Holocaust remembering, though it does require some research to bring this versatility to the surface.[4] A parallel can be drawn with urban planners in Emmen who concentrated on modernist construction without losing sight of the inclusion of prevailing landscape elements such as relief, dolmen or residual farms. The surrounding landscape had to penetrate the modern residential areas, as the chief urban planner described his ideal. A slightly elevated street in New Town Emmen could conceal a ridge created by boulder clay carried from the land ice, 150,000 years ago. The same could be said of the immaterial past. In this respect, Emmen offers a fitting introduction to the landscape of memory in the 1950s, a period in which the Holocaust, as it is now understood, was not yet part of public discourse, but in which seemingly incidental performative acts might leave indelible impressions. A Greek tragedy performed by pupils of a grammar school could thus summon up more recent horrors of war.

After the war, the municipal lyceum was opened to students who wished to take a classical education, including Latin and Greek. Children of peat workers became first-generation lyceum pupils. The school was housed in a temporary timber structure, but included a classical portico, with its distinctive columns, pediment and peristyle. In front of the school was a fountain where the music-making forest god Pan resided. An auditorium was built next to the school to support the civilizing strategy.[5]

To celebrate the opening of the auditorium, the talented writer Harry Mulisch was invited. It wouldn't be long before he successfully remodeled himself as the literary voice of WWII, but that wasn't yet the case when traveling to Emmen. Mulisch was born in 1927 from parents living in exile. His father grew up in Bielitz, near Auschwitz, which was part of the Austrian part of the Danube Monarchy. He came to live in the Netherlands after WWI, where he met his wife, born from a Frankfurt Jewish family. In WWII, father collaborated with the German forces but made sure that mother and son weren't deported. The author summed it up in the aphorism that he was born from WWI and embodied WWII. In 1957, Harry Mulisch was the first recipient of the Anne Frank Prize that the Hacketts initiated on the basis of their script's royalties. One year later he was appointed as a jury member and 30 years later he confessed that he had only started reading Anne's diary because of an invitation to the presentation of the critical edition in 1986.[6]

In January 1954, the young writer was on his way to Emmen, sharing his travel experiences with the readers of an intellectual weekly. 'The old locomotive groaned, pulling its dusty carts . . . through the ancient land of Stone Age man and bog corpses . . . until the end of the world.' Arriving dusty and tired, Germany turned out to be alarmingly close. 'God forbid!' But what a surprise. The scales fell from his eyes. Once a desert, Emmen had been transformed into an oasis of modern architecture. The auditorium exceeded Mulisch's wildest expectations.

In the first week of September 1955, the school staged *Trojan Women* in the same auditorium. This play by the ancient Greek playwright Euripides told of the aftermath of the Greco-Trojan War when all male Trojans have been killed and the remaining women are to be taken as spoils of war. The teachers had managed to get Karl Guttmann, who was employed by the prominent theater ensemble *De Haagse Comedie*, to travel up north and direct just under 30 pupils for three performances – one year before he directed the Anne Frank play.

Two hundred kilometers seems a short distance; but for the centrally organized Dutch theater world, it was unheard of to cross the threshold to 'the province,' let alone Drenthe. Jules Croiset, who would take on the role of Peter when the company passed Emmen on March 18, 1957, still remembers the intimate auditorium, but also the long two-lane road to it and the even longer journey back.[7] Mulisch wasn't the only visitor who thought no further than dolmen and peat. Cultural decentralization, 'to make up for the tremendous underconsumption of theater,' had only just begun. In the north, authorities joined forces to 'bring culture to the uneducated masses' and anticipate an undesirable exodus from the rural provinces. But that turned out to be not that simple. After a first 'not entirely successful' attempt at establishing modern theater in the north, a second effort came from the more southern town of Arnhem. Rob de Vries's ensemble was pulled out of the mud to become the proverbial white raven of cultural decentralization, thanks to Rob's strong belief in the need of overthrowing the cultural hegemony of the West.[8]

The pioneering role for Emmen lay in a modernization policy propelled by a far from provincial elite. At the time, the lyceum was blessed with highly learned instructors some of whom belonged to the world top in their specialties. One of them was Hendrik Joan Drossaart Lulofs, professor of Classical Culture at the University of Amsterdam and specialist in the textual transfer of Aristotle through Greek, Syrian, Arabic, Hebrew and Latin. Lulofs was responsible for the smooth translation of the Euripides script. A few months before, stage director Guttmann had directed *The Trojan War Will Not Take Place* (1935) by French playwright Jean Giraudoux on the occasion of the prestigious Holland festival. Two student ensembles had preceded Guttmann. This was not remarkable because interest in ancient Greek theater had mainly come from students with the establishment of gymnasiums at the end of the nineteenth century. Professional productions only began after WWI.[9] Giraudoux's play was a nice variation, albeit with less tragedy and more irony than the surviving ancient tragedies. The threat of war that hung like a dark cloud over Europe had inspired the playwright to write a counterfactual narrative of that most infamous war story of all time. What if Hector had managed to avert the threat of war with Greece after the elopement of Helen? Not only would we never have known about the ruse with the wooden horse, but neither would the tragedy of manslaughter and destruction have occurred. This was all ludic and performative ruminating, of course, since Homer had left us a fictional drama to which the French playwright responded with an equally imaginative prequel. Amid threats implicated in the Cold War, many acknowledged its urgency: 'The topicality of this disturbing play is almost claustrophobic,' Guttmann observed.[10]

'An antique text is a piece of life that can be relived playfully,' was the directive teacher Lulofs tried to live by.[11] This seems to echo the more widespread revival of Euripides in the early part of the twentieth century. It was still a relatively new understanding that an ancient play was not just a classicist's study object but for everyone to enjoy in an actual performance. Around WWI, Euripides was transformed into a contemporary playwright whose work resonates in modern times.[12] And so ten years after the ending of the war, the tragedy about the fate of exile and dead that struck the Trojan women, which Euripides wrote in light of his own experiences with the protracted Peloponnesian War, was chosen to celebrate a restored Dutch–German friendship in the postwar border region. The performance hit a nerve in more than one way. This was about seeing your daughters and sons on the school stage, about high culture in the far north and about reaching out to the guests from across the border. But sometimes a play functions as a séance in which some uninvited ghosts are awakened, as remnants of the past: those that cling to the characters, to the actors' lives, their previous roles or to the performance site.[13] Guttmann was thus heartened by the locals who 'had responded intensely to the deportation of innocent women, which took place 3,000 years ago and was described 2,500 years ago.'[14] One cannot fail to think that his words were an invocation to events that had taken place a little further on.

Trojan Women premiered simultaneously with the US premiere of the Anne Frank play, October 1955. The Broadway play was a major commercial and critical success and that did not go unnoticed in the Netherlands. In fact, Rob de Vries was already busy obtaining the performing rights. We don't know if at the time Guttmann publicly discussed the parallels between *Trojan Women* and the Anne Frank play, but he certainly did so 30 years later. In 1984, the director attended the premiere of the second major production of the Hacketts script, this time under the direction of Jeroen Krabbé. When asked to compare the two productions, Guttmann retorted:

> Do you happen to know Euripides's *Trojan Women*? That play is about the deportation of Trojan women from their home country. Euripides's account is heart-breaking, including lamentation and choirs. That was such a liberating play at the time. The same cathartic effect has had the first staging of *The Diary of Anne Frank* in the Netherlands.[15]

The journalist did not inquire further, so we are left with the intriguing observation that the director was referring to a play staged 30 years earlier in a small town in-the-making to express the affective impact of the Anne Frank play. In itself, references to classical tragedy were not uncommon when discussing the play, for example when a critic elaborated on the role of fate, tyche, in Ancient Greece.[16] But this went further.

Theater in Drenthe produced an affective turn as captured in the well-known drama concept of catharsis – introduced by Aristotle in his *Poetics* (fourth century BC) – similar to the one experienced by critic Tynan in Berlin. In 1957, an attempt was made to erect a monument in Westerbork commemorating the Jewish victims 'to express humility and silence instead of vanity and haughtiness.' At a fundraising event, provincial governor Jacob Cramer addressed sponsors and Israel's ambassador: 'After the performance of "The Diary of Anne Frank," the audience leaves the venue silent and calm, with a sense of sorrow and shame.' Silence connected play and monument; silence not as a lack but as an expression of empathy, as the governor clarified. There will be those who continue to be haunted by a sense of shame and guilt. This might well be because we had not shown enough solidarity, 'were too focused on self-preservation, and therefore insufficiently aware of the agony of others.' So here we come across an early public manifestation of empathy:

> Drenthe was the province with a very high percentage of Jews, I need only mention Assen . . . and the village of Emmen. . . . We have seen their children play in our streets in innocence and childish candor. They have disappeared from our provincial society but their presence cannot be unseen. . . . Add to this the close presence of the Jewish camp.[17]

These were remarkable words of mourning for local Jewish communities that found recognition through the absent children. Affective rhetoric (shame, anxiety, guilt) came attached to the camp and the victims in the Drenthe communities. It is this chain of signifiers, from Anne to the children who couldn't be seen or unseen, that went against 'an indolence of the heart' – or *acedia* as one of the deadly sins – and aroused, as Walter Benjamin put it, an *identification affective*.[18]

In the 1950s, the Anne Frank play became part of a chain of performative acts that foregrounded the Westerbork camp and the Shoah. These acts, through the combined effort and the circulation of familiar and lesser known signs, resulted in an early sense of empathy and the recognition of a loss. A turn in the public acknowledgment of the Shoah is usually situated in the years of the 1961 Eichmann trial or the 1965 publication of *Ashes in the Wind: The Destruction of Dutch Jewry* by Dutch historian (and former teacher of Anne), Jacques Presser. Or perhaps much later, in the late 1970s, when the American series *Holocaust* appeared on Dutch television or when young Jews began to raise their voices. Among them was Jeroen Krabbé who decided on a new production of the Anne Frank play in 1983 and among them was actor Jules Croiset as one of the protesters against the staging of Rainer Werner Fassbinder's play *Garbage, the City and Death* in 1987.

The governor's speech must be combined with the staging and the efforts to erect a monument to assess its full impact. In the latter case, he encountered objections from some Jewish survivors who no longer wanted to stand out for fear of repetition or shame or who dismissed a monument as a tasteless spectacle 'to gaze at.' Indeed, similar objections were raised with respect to the play. The monument never left the drawing board.[19]

Harry Mulisch, whose oeuvre according to his carefully constructed image coincides with 'the war,' referred in his travelogue to all the clichés of Drenthe's history, but without referencing Westerbork. The Shoah didn't appear in his fiction either at the time. In April 1956, he visited the Institute for War Documentation for the first time to research a novel. *The Stone Bridal Bed* (*Het stenen bruidsbed*, 1959), the book he handed in after winning the Anne Frank Prize, is a literary reflection on the ruins of Dresden and included explicit references to the ruins of Troy. The protagonist is an American pilot who had participated in the bombing of the German city and who, spectrally, self-identifies as 'a Greek who died under Agamemnon, but is still alive.' A few years later, Mulisch published *Criminal Case 40/61* (*De zaak 40/61. Een reportage*, 1962) on the Eichmann trial. It was only in his great celestial novel, *The Discovery of Heaven* (*De ontdekking van de hemel*, 1992) that he turned to the ruins of Westerbork and Auschwitz, interlinking and inscribing both sites in a universal history. The novel included a scene at the modest monument that was finally built in 1970 – Rob de Vries being one of the early initiators: curved railway lines leading to heaven against a wall of Ice Age boulders (which slow but steady 'work themselves to the surface from the depths,' as Mulisch put it). The novel is about the circumvention of time and the ubiquity of the past. The protagonist is an astronomer who, being born from an Austrian father (from Bielitz-Auschwitz) and a Jewish mother (sent to Auschwitz), ends up working in Westerbork. The site is by then, because of the placement of 14 parabolic antennas, transformed into a typical Mulisch-like place if you have an eye for the confluence of the temporary stay of the starred prisoners and the eternal celestial stars.

It is as if the Westerbork site and Mulisch slowly converged. Only after all remains of the camp had been erased, a museum was established. Years later, the absence of material traces led to the search for one of the barracks. Everything was sold to neighboring farmers when the site was cleared. Yet one structure was found intact and this happened to be the block in which the Frank family was incarcerated. Just when the shed was about to be retransferred, a fire broke out and nothing remained, except for some footage that was shot for the film adaptation of Mulisch's novel. Inside, the astronomer has an epiphany about the location of heaven and then, by divine intercession, is hit by a meteorite. The director was Krabbé, the screenwriter was Rob's son Edwin de Vries. The history of the camp, the family history of De Vries and the oeuvre of Mulisch signal a process in which sites, bodies and artifacts were cited and aligned, creating an affective topography of the Shoah, with Anne Frank as one of the key signs.

The governor of Drenthe had acknowledged his accountability. Involved in setting up the refugee camp, he came to feel implicated in the next fatal steps. His words point to a side effect of a theatrical 'catharsis': an ethical shift, that is, an empathic reassessment of the self in relation to an other.[20]

Bialik's last words

> And heavy your life will be
> Such long nights and not one star
> Your groans will vanish in the wind
> And to your call, God won't listen.[21]

In 1903, the poet Hayim Nahman Bialik envisioned a starless night when he came face to face with the antisemitic atrocities in the Russian territories, as a young Karl Guttmann would recall in 1934 when a new wave of violence unfolded. Another two decades later, the Anne Frank play fulfilled a role similar to the reciting of Bialik's poem, this time evoking the wave of violence to which Karl and his family were exposed. It is more than likely that the catharsis to which the director was referring when addressing the play affected not only the audience but also himself.

Karl Guttmann was born in 1913 in the town of Drohobych near Lviv in Galicia, the region that alternately was part of Poland, Austria, Russia and Ukraine.[22] When he was a toddler, his parents fled hundreds of miles west to the town of Bielitz as a precaution against impending violence. Bielitz is situated on the border of Silesia and Galicia and, like Drohobych, fell under the sovereignty of the Austrian branch of the Danube Monarchy. In the predominantly rural world of Galicia, tufts of industrialization – oil in Drohobych, textiles in Bielitz – coexisted with the modern trade. Yet craftsmen, small shop owners and peddlers felt the burden of economic change, many of whom were Jewish. Structural poverty and socioeconomic transformations went hand in hand with antisemitic agitation. At the end of the century, a wave of pogroms swept through the region. Jews faced a permanent threat and the West – from Central Europe to distant America – was beckoning. Between 1880 and 1914, 350,000 Jews emigrated from Galicia.[23] Compared to Drohobych that suffered from political unrest and antisemitic incidents, Bielitz was a peaceful oasis. It became the place where Karl grew up, but also where he had to flee from the Nazis and to which he returned at the end of his life to say kaddish, the prayer for the dead, at the remains of the broken synagogue.

The first Jews to settle in Bielitz were a tax inspector and his family. This was at the end of the seventeenth century when legal equality was still a long way off. A century later, three families had joined.[24] The Jewish presence was only really noticed in the course of the nineteenth century when emancipation in German-speaking Europe drew people from afar. The boom in the local economy had the same effect. The Jewish population increased to several thousand and the community received permission to build a place of worship. In 1881, the largest temple in the area was erected. The synagogue on Tempelstrasse symbolized the prosperity that Jews had acquired in the textile industry and trade but also radiated the modern architectural urbanity in fin-de-siècle Bielitz.

The local middle class modeled after German-speaking Europe. Guttmann's grandparents had their roots in a world where Yiddish, the language of Eastern European Jewry, prevailed. His parents tried to move away from these roots because, like so many, they sought assimilation and thus a new interpretation of their Jewishness. Hence the focus on German-speaking culture. Different forms of European Judaism coexisted in Bielitz. Newcomers may have visited the more traditional shul first and later transferred to the liberal synagogue on Tempelstrasse. On the other side of the river, a community adhering to Hasidism lived in the sister city of Biala. This is the religious revival faith that was popular in Galicia and which included Karl's maternal family from Brody.

After WWI, national borders shifted across Europe and new states were created. The territory around Bielitz, including neighboring Kraków, was added to Poland. Bielitz became Bielsko, but Karl would stick to the former place name for the rest of his life. With the impending policy of Polonization, Jewish assimilationists who were centered on German culture were left empty-handed. More was to follow. Nationalism, xenophobia and antisemitic politics would be vociferous in the late 1920s – Karl's school years – and violent incidents on the streets increased.

Combining a mixture of religious and secular education, Karl attended the Jewish Cheider school for teaching the precepts of the faith and liturgical Hebrew, followed by the public German gymnasium. In 1931, he enrolled in a commercial business college in Vienna. As an additional income, the young student started to participate in public recitations, with which he had already achieved some success in Bielitz. In 1934, a poem by Hayim Nahman Bialik, who died that year, was on his program for the Jewish student association.

Das Letzte Wort – in the Yiddish original *Dos letste vort* – dealt with the pogrom of 1903 in Kishinev or, as the city is now known, Chisinau, in Bessarabia near the Black Sea. This three-day devastating slaughter of rape, murder and looting was not the first in the bordered settlement for millions of Russian Jews. It was however the first of the new century and one that had thrown the worldwide Jewish community into commotion. The pogrom took place in a week when the end of the Passover celebrations coincided with Easter, the ideal time to rekindle the time-honored false antisemitic allegation of ritual murder and lust for Christian blood. Forty-nine people died – more than in the preceding pogroms added up.[25] After the pogrom, Bialik took the remarkable step of traveling from Odessa to Chisinau to collect testimonies. Also new was the wave of literature, poetry and theater that followed in the wake of the pogrom. In the words of historian David G.

Roskies, a new phase in the Jewish 'Literature of Destruction' set in. This label pertains to the literary recordings of the persecutions – with destruction, once referring to the destruction of the temples in classical times, becoming a common term in early testimonies of what ultimately became known as the Shoah. Thirty years later, Guttmann was able to recite his poem because of the collective memory that arose on this collection of literary responses.[26]

The Jewish destruction literature linked experiences of violence with the Hebrew Bible, with the history and myth of exile and persecution as well as with histories of resilience and resurrection. This time the covenantal trust in God had been hit hard, as Bialik made abundantly clear in his 'poetry of rage': 'And to your call, God won't listen,' the poet exclaimed in Guttmann's recitation. New was the way in which both revenge and resistance were called for in literature as in real life: less passive victimization and more decisive action were needed. Self-defense groups emerged referencing heroic mythic-historical moments such as the successful battle of the Maccabees in 167 BC against the rulers of Judea, the Greek-speaking Syrians, as recorded in the *Book of the Maccabees* and celebrated with Hanukkah.

Bialik was celebrated as the patriarch of Hebrew poetry and in 1931 the *grosse hebraïsche Dichter* visited Bielitz. Two years later, the Bialik House was opened next to the synagogue. However, a year after Hitler's seizure of power, Guttmann's recitation was more than a tribute to Bialik. It was part of a Jewish memory culture. In retrospect, it did not bode well. The sociopolitical climate was changing. The German-speaking population had set up its own local Nazi department; antisemitic propaganda, harassment and vandalism increased from Polish and German sides.

The young student was familiar with Jewish literature, German drama and classical culture; he had yet to become a theater practitioner. Karl always had a fascination for drama. As a little boy, he regularly sneaked into Bielitz's municipal theater to enjoy its otherworldliness, later doing so with the janitor's permission.[27] Now once in Vienna, his recitations were noticed by a drama critic and so, on his recommendation, he was admitted at the theater school of the famous director Max Reinhardt.

After graduating in 1935, under direction of Otto Preminger, Guttmann returned to Bielitz's municipal theater as *Jugendlicher Held und Charakterliebhaber*. This included roles he could not have obtained as a Jew in Vienna. Yet his career was stalled by the *Anschluss*, the union of Germany and Austria in 1938. Jewish artists were expelled and Guttmann turned to the vibrant ensemble of Ostrava in the Czech Republic. 'At some point,' as he recalls, 'they also no longer wanted Jews in large, positive roles either [in Bielitz or Ostrava].' A year later war broke out.

Two days after the invasion, German troops occupied Bielitz. The synagogue and the Bialik center were set on fire. One part of the Jewish population fled east, the rest were terrorized and sent to a camp near Lublin or to one of the newly established ghettos in Kraków and Będzin. Guttmann's brother Julius was killed. On June 20, 1942, more than 400 people were transported from the ghetto in Bielitz to the town of Auschwitz, 30 km away and known by townspeople from short holidays and shopping visits.[28]

The German invasion destroyed a Jewish world built up over two centuries. The city – nicknamed Little Vienna – was culturally orientated toward the metropole with a theater where the bourgeoisie was nourished by Goethe and Schiller – to which the Germans added Shakespeare. This was the cultural heritage that Guttmann would propagate in the Netherlands and with which Otto Frank was familiar and which he passed on to Anne while in hiding. The Jewish community was committed to providing social services for the poor. Karl had been a member of the Jewish Boy Scout. Survivors who spent their youth in Bielitz especially praised the atmosphere of competitive sports. The water polo team was renowned and the town housed the region's very first Maccabi gymnastics club, named after the ancient Maccabees. The sporting atmosphere was partly the result of the ubiquitous nationalist sportiness of the late nineteenth century, a great nation in a healthy body, that had spilled over from Germany to the Czech Republic and Poland. Inspired by this, a climate developed among Jews to turn centuries of subordination into muscle and resilience.[29] This movement was thus part of a widespread re-translation of the Jewish body and spirit that also included reform of the theater as pursued by Reinhardt: more movement, more spectacle, more energetic, and less textual, while 'offering new models of what it means to act "Jewish".'[30]

On September 1, 1939, Karl Guttmann fled to Lviv, a city invaded by Russia. Gutmann reunited with his father and sister, his mother had died of natural causes in 1938, and married a young woman named Kitty Wachtl from his hometown. Then followed a vital encounter with Alter Kacyzne, poet, photographer and theater practitioner. Kacyzne gave Karl a golden tip: 'Lern Yiddish!' Indeed, the Russians in Lviv preferred Yiddish rather than Hebrew, the language they simultaneously saw as reactionary and as vehicle for Zionist nationalism. As was customary in these parts, Karl grew up with some familiarity with Yiddish – the language was 'in his ears' – because of his parents.

In 1941, he seemed to be able to recite his way through the war with texts by poets such as Itzik Manger and Yisroel Ashendorf. Then the German army finally advanced to Lviv and because Karl was in Kiev for a recital, he was cut off from his family. Only much later did he learn that Kitty was left behind by the retreating Russian troops and got killed in the unfolding pogrom. Guttmann moved on, thousands of miles further east in the direction of Tashkent: eventually ending up in Iraq – where he had a Passover celebration with local people – and, in the wake of a Polish allied army created on Russian soil, traveling on to Palestine. There he united with his father and sister, began to learn the trade of weaver and very soon joined a theater ensemble.

By now the Jewish destruction literature could be supplemented with new poetry, literature and theater. Here in this time and even before the official end of WWII, a corpus of testimonies, diaries, memoirs and literature arose that came to be read, edited and played under the heading of Holocaust literature and theater.

Staged heroism

In the summer of 1942, actor Robert de Vries pulled a great stunt. Or, so it seemed afterward. At the time, it was a bold act of defiance. Twenty years later, in the same week that *The Diary of Anne Frank* aired on Dutch television, he was given the opportunity to recount his adventure as a driver of the Westerbork mail train on prime time television. Sitting in a comfy chair, De Vries revealed the events of the great escape from Westerbork, almost like a trickster's tall tale. 'There was this girl [captured in Westerbork] . . . she was a Jewish girl. And so I said: "I don't think I should continue working until that girl is out."'[31] De Vries traveled to Drenthe where he convinced the chief engineer of the mail train to join in his audacious plan. The train with secondhand De Vries – soot on his cheeks, cap on his head, handkerchief casually out of his pocket – literally drove into the camp to deliver the mail. Only this time Hannelore Cahn would hide under a few bags after which the train quietly drove out of the camp. Mission accomplished. And so it went, even if only after Hannelore slept on it.

Although they reached Amsterdam safely, there was a catch to this happy ending as became clear when a documentary was made that gave Hannelore an opportunity to give her side of the story. At the age of 83, the love of *Westerbork Girl* Hannelore did not seem have diminished: 'It was just Rob and I. I liked him, I think he was a very good-looking guy. Very male, absolutely.'[32] The camp commander felt his honor had been tarnished and a search team was installed. Hannelore was well-known among the inmates as one of the cabaret dancing girls and, being fond of Hannelore, one man traveled to Amsterdam and managed to track her down. A complicated triangular relationship unfolded. Rob and Hannelore were in love, but the first had no time for her. Hannelore felt lost and somehow yearned back to Westerbork while she also felt the pressure from the man who would be punished with deportation if she did not return. A dramatic moment unfolded on the tram. The three got into a discussion that got so heated that 'a stranger,' as Hannelore recalls, sought to expose Rob as a Jew. They quickly broke up. Hannelore, indeed, returned to Westerbork. Back in the camp, the commander pressed her to marry the man who brought her back. The couple survived the war and moved to America.

The remarkable escape endorsed Rob's status as a romantic and fearless resistance hero, utterly masculine, a status he effectively used in the roles he was to play onstage and on-screen until his early death at the age of 51. A striking example is a newsreel of a New Year's wish in December 1945. Five artists recited a poem and De Vries was set to do his part against the backdrop of a maritime scenery wearing a woolen sailor jersey.[33]

> Fearless lads, sturdy chaps
> Yes, we are ready to act
> We are young and well-made
> Equipped for the New Year
> We want to build and work
> For more prosperity and authority
> Make way and put your trust in us
> Raise the banner

Everyone in the Netherlands will have understood the redundant archaic signs. 'Fearless lads, sturdy chaps' (*Stoere jongens/ferme knapen*) is the language of nineteenth-century nationalism, from textbooks, children's stories and uplifting melodies, referring to the maritime heroes, explorers and traders who made the Dutch Republic a prime world economy. But the most obvious sign was Rob de Vries, the young man who radiated courage, and of whom you knew that if he represented the best of his generation, everything would turn out fine in the country. Or, as one of his companions in the resistance felt on their first meeting: this man is not just in the resistance, he plays being at it. 'I thought this can't be a good actor.'[34]

At the time Robert de Vries, born Abraham in 1918, was 27 years old. In his late teens, he had renounced his orthodox upbringing only to move out of religion altogether. During the occupation, he was classified as Jewish all the same. He was rejected from drama school at the age of 17 ('malaise,' he noted melodramatically in an autobiographical note), attended night school and found an office job. Meanwhile, he took private acting lessons. And successfully so. At the start of the war, he obtained a part in an old theater hit along with two members of the future cast of the Anne Frank play.[35] When the occupiers pursued a policy to exclude 'Jews' from the profession, he joined the Jewish Kleinkunst Ensemble of German entertainer Rudolf Nelson. The ensemble was allowed to play just until the deportations took off, July 1942. Many cast members were deported and killed (including Willy Rosen and Kurt Gerron), Rob went into hiding. Enny Mols-De Leeuwe, the future Mrs. Van Daan, was personally protected by her 'mixed marriage.'

De Vries became active in a resistance group whose specialty was to forge identity cards and food stamps. Rob was always in for action, delivering parcels, armed when needed, 'a young artist with a great imagination and an equally great humor, who had a childlike pleasure in disguises.' A number of members were arrested. De Vries was among them, but it was partly, thanks to his ID card that he was identified as non-Jewish. If we go by the memoirs written in the mode of an adventure story that his companion published, Rob remained fearless: when they both 'fell into the clutches of the Gestapo,' De Vries was 'chained to an armchair' but he 'would rather be torn to pieces' than betray his friends. In fact, 'his tale was so ingenious that De Vries left the Germans no other option than to acquit him.'[36] Eventually De Vries was imprisoned for a year and a half in camp Vught followed by three other prisons after which he was released in September 1944 when it was believed the country would be liberated any moment. But that did not happen. During the 1944–1945 famine, De Vries took shelter with a diverse group of people, including a future prime minister, in a residential block near the Jewish quarter, discussing the ideal contours of the postwar world.

Resistance was extremely serious for Rob, but that didn't get in the way of masquerades and make-believe. Images of fierce male resistance were stuck to Rob, yet something about his image of archetypical hero remains ambiguous. Everything seems to show that he was fearless on stage like in real life. But there are some signs that suggest otherwise. Nor did his position seem entirely consistent with the dominant image of the modest, even reserved, role of the small community of Jews. He was more like the 'new Jew' who was primed in the movement of muscular Judaism: self-conscious, masculine and tough. But then again, perhaps he had maintained as little of his Jewishness from when he had explicitly renounced his Orthodox upbringing. You start to wonder if the audience knew that De Vries was Jewish at all. Or at least whether they knew that a man codified by the Nazis as such had fearlessly entered Westerbork to rescue a Jewish girl. That would have been a great story to counter the classic stereotype of the cowardly Jew who leaves the fight to others that circulated among former resistance fighters in the postwar years.

De Vries died in 1969 at the start of a series of performances of the Euripides play *Hippolytos*. The dismay was great. People gathered to pay the actor the last honor. Numerous obits appeared yet without referencing his Jewish roots whatsoever. But then again, who decides whether if and how to be Jewish, particularly after the war, and who's to say what may count as the right mode of Jewishness? At one point in the footage on the great escape from Westerbork, Hannelore told Rob's son Edwin about the incident on the tram when she hesitated about returning to the camp, revealing that 'the stranger' had even called on Rob 'to drop his pants.' Edwin immediately responded: 'Oh, that was the big fear of my father, that they found out about his Jewishness.' Of course that was true for all people that tried to hide their origins at a time of fierce persecution. But Rob's son referred to a disturbing postwar sentiment, as a surviving scrap with autobiographical notes suggests: Born 'from J parents,' in the war 'outlawed – nameless – ignorance – fear.'[37] Instead of unparalleled fearlessness, we come across an anxiety that lingered after the war. Rob's choice of secularism and assimilation – as it was called in prewar terms – was then reinforced by the fear of repetition, as his son explained:

> We learned nothing about Jewish culture at home. We did not celebrate the Jewish holidays, we did not become a Bar-Mitzvah, we were not circumcised, because then you could possibly be recognized as a Jew. That was my father's great fear.

Still he 'always pointed out who the "real Jews" were' or where to find the best Jewish delicatessen': hesitantly Jewish but a survivor nevertheless. Thus, as his son continued, 'I came to realize we received an education that was clearly orthodox, in morals, that is.'[38] There was a constant undertone of anxiety and heedfulness. Ten years after the liberation, the diary dramatization would serve as an ideal vehicle to cast these affects in a dramatic form.

Working through the past

'He who seeks to approach his own buried past must conduct himself like a man digging.'[39] In *The Discovery of Heaven*, Harry Mulisch offered an understanding of history termed a philosophy of homologies 'that is at odds with the linear and causal interpretation of reality' and, if necessary, contains aspects that would superficially be seen as contradictions. In this perspective, Westerbork and Auschwitz 'echo or rhyme significantly with each other,' as JM Coetzee stressed in his review, just as Homeric violence apprises a twentieth-century genocide. Such a theory of temporal coincidences, spatial citations and versatile simultaneities is more than the conventional conception of memory can hold, yet that is quite common in theater – as the examples of Euripides and Bialik, among others, show. Striking is the relationship to Walter Benjamin's notion of time in which the past is 'seized as an image that flashes up at the moment of its recognizability and is never seen again.' It is in the arts, and this monograph is about drama first and foremost, where this non-chronological and non-progressive sense of time – the result of a poetic mnemonic act – is most palpable.[40]

Shoah references remained 'submerged and subliminal,' yet surfaced in a Greek school play – as they did in *The Diary of Anne Frank*. What about the flashes of a recent past in early postwar theater? What dramatic models were available to create a theater of the Shoah in the ten years leading up to the Anne Frank play? Mention was made of a national heroic model, following in the footsteps of a chronological, modernizing time frame, and of a tragic cyclical model of Jewish destruction, accentuating the reiteration and reappearance of loss.

As elsewhere in Europe, in the Netherlands the war mainly took on significance as a liberation from foreign occupation. The hegemonic nationalist and heroic tenor was in agreement with what would become the commemorative narrative: how 'we' had overcome tyranny, thanks to the courageous work of the resistance. Similar praise befell the Dutch theater community which, broadly speaking, had not lend itself to Nazi propaganda – or so it was said. 'Long live the theater! Long live freedom!' New plays focused on propagating this narrative.

On the very first day of the liberation, a group of theater practitioners who had refused cooperation with the Nazis unambiguously took possession of the Amsterdam municipal theater; and Rob was there that day. Theater practitioners who had continued working for whatever reason were punished with a temporary ban. A transition ensemble aptly named *May 5, 1945* set to rehearse a play entitled *Free Folk*.[41] The excitement among the 50 actors and directors was great and the tone solemn. The play's focus was on five key moments of resistance and liberation in Dutch history. According to the playwrights, the linear history play was the most suitable form to celebrate independence and freedom. Rob signed for two roles. The last act mainly took place in two prison cells. The prisoners, coming from all walks of life, were united in their fight against the German occupiers. The Jewish perspective was missing, although there is one dialogue about the 'Jewish Dutch' who were murdered 'simply because they exist.' In a play that followed soon after, *The Nameless of 1942*, Rob got the perfect role, that of a son who transfers stolen identity cards to the resistance.[42] The play was about a family whose father is the only one of Jewish descent, but the persecution offered little more than the backdrop to the real drama of the arrest and execution of one of the sons in the resistance.

A different note came from the Jewish Weekly, which already called on the theater world in March 1946 to take up its plight. If theater is to take itself seriously, 'the Jewish problem' must be visualized on stage and the supply has been poor so far.[43] An attempt was made via two plays by Franz Werfel. De Haagse Comedie staged *Jakubowsky und der Oberst*, a tragi-comic story on a classic Jewish subject – persecution and flight. The script was recited by Guttmann in Palestine. Rob's tutor Albert van Dalsum retook Werfel's prewar play *Paulus under den Juden* (1926) to deliver 'an upper-cut to the antisemites' and, thematizing antisemitism, *Home of the Brave* by Arthur Laurents with De Vries in a lead role.[44] The Jewish Weekly was most passionate about a monologue performed by Enny Mols. *Farewell* told the story of a Jewish prisoner, her prewar life, life in the ghetto, going into hiding and work in the resistance: 'This is the most striking rendition of our suffering to date.'[45] The small Eastern European Yiddish Association restored its activities with annual commemorations of the *Hurbn* and the Warsaw Ghetto Uprising. This included recitation, music and theater, a play by Chaim Sloves or a recitation by Ernst Deutsch, the Jewish actor who would play the parts of Shylock, Nathan and Otto Frank in postwar German theater.

Meanwhile, Guttmann learned to act in Modern Hebrew. He joined the influx of migrants who wanted to play modern European theater – different from the more traditional style of Habima. Kameri became his new company.[46] This also corresponded with the role for Palestine as a benchmark for a new Jewishness, one that was not grafted on an ancient past or on European 'acquiescence' but instead insisted on a vital future in the new land. The latter vision was also what put Karl and Rob in touch.

After the first euphoric months in liberation, Rob joined an ensemble that went for the Dutch classics but also staged the first *Death of a Salesman.* In 1949, the ensemble took up *The Ring and the Kilim*, a play by the young Dutch playwright Luisa Treves. On a press assignment to Israel, she went after her script which, as it turned out, had ended up with the dramatist of the Kameri theater, Karl Guttmann. To cut a long story short. The two fell in love, got married and moved to the Netherlands.[47] As a Dutch director made preparations for a production of *The Ring and the Kilim* with the Kameri ensemble, Karl warned him not to stage it as a comedy like 'his friend' De Vries had done in the Netherlands. In Israel, the subject would be too sensitive to do so.[48]

The drama is a ludic blend of ancient and modern times, testifying to the ubiquity of the past, or rather the drive to excavate the present, as Benjamin put it. The main character is a young Polish-Jewish woman who, after having experienced the concentration camps, is on Cyprus waiting for a transfer to Palestine. Meanwhile, archaeological excavations are taking place. At one point, an excavated ring flashes the story back to ancient times when the island was occupied by the Persians.

The play revolved around understanding mass violence, either as a time- and place-related disaster or as a universal burden for humanity. For the young woman in limbo, the kilim at the same time acts as a reminder of her past in Poland and her future in Palestine. The ring, on the other hand, symbolizes that suffering and empathy transcend time and place. Or, as the author explained in a side note: 'We haven't behaved as well as humans in recent years, and we, who have acted wrongly, and we who had to endure it, want to forget as soon as possible.' But is it possible to start over without considering the shards of the past? Digging up those shards – a ring, or a diary for that matter – is one thing, but what to do with it is key. After all, the dramatic effect of being transported back in time can be funny, but, as illustrated by Guttmann's cautionary remark, a dramatic confrontation with the past can also transform in a deeply disturbing endeavor.

Notes

1 G.L. Durlacher, *Quarantaine* (Amsterdam, 1994), 16–17.
2 Andy Pearce, *Holocaust consciousness in contemporary Britain* (New York, 2014), 2.
3 C.J.M. Schuyt and E. Verberne, *1950: Welvaart in zwart-wit* (Den Haag, 2000), 39.
4 Michael Rothberg, *Multidirectional memory: Remembering the Holocaust in the age of decolonization* (Stanford, 2009).
5 On Drenthe, see: Dirkje Mulder-Boers, *De grens getrokken: Noord-Nederlandse grensbewoners tussen 1914–1964* (Assen, 2020); 'Het wonder Emmen', *Andere Tijden*, NPO TV, February 20, 2016, www.anderetijden.nl; conversation with local historian Sis Hoek, Emmen, July 15, 2020, who kindly handed me a copy of the school jubilee booklet *Vijftig Jaar GSG Emmen.*
6 Harry Mulisch, *Voer voor psychologen* (Amsterdam, 1960); *De Groene Amsterdammer*, January 23, 1954; 'Death and the Maiden,' *The New York Review of Books*, July 17, 1986 (lecture April 6, 1986, *Akademie der Künste*, Berlin); LM: 231 Mulisch Archive, 334.4b Correspondence, 1956–1964.
7 Interview Ensel – Croiset, August 8, 2020.
8 GA 0644, 8: correspondence company board, 1955–1956; GA 0644, 9: overview of Theater in the first three years of its existence (October 25, 1956).
9 *Er komt geen oorlog met Troje*, premiere June 15, 1955; René Veenman, *De klassieke traditie in de Lage Landen* (Nijmegen, 2009), 295.
10 *Algemeen Dagblad*, June 11, 1955.
11 H. Daiber, 'Levensbericht H.J. Drossaart Lulofs,' in *KNAW, Levensberichten en herdenkingen* (Amsterdam, 2000), 11–16.
12 Gilbert Murray, *Euripides and his age* (New York, 1913) was especially influential.
13 Marvin Carlson, *The haunted stage: The theatre as memory machine* (Ann Arbor, 2001).
14 *Het Vrije Volk*, November 19, 1955.
15 Interviews in *NIW*, February 24, 1984; May 22, 1992.
16 *Die Welt*, October 2, 1956.

17 *Nieuwsblad van het Noorden*, November 1, 1957; *NIW*, November 8, 1957.
18 Walter Benjamin, 'On the concept of history,' in *Fire alarm: Reading Walter Benjamin's "On the concept of history"*, ed. Michael Löwy (London, 2016), 46–57 (thesis VII).
19 On the opposition, see: *Algemeen Handelsblad*, January 13, 1957; *de Volkskrant*, January 9, 1966.
20 Michael Rothberg, *The implicated subject: Beyond victims and perpetrators* (Stanford, 2019).
21 Hayyim Nahman Bialik, 'Dos letste vort,' *Sami Rohr Library of Yiddish Audio Books*, www.archiv.org (translation: re); Chaïm Nachman Bialik, *Gedichte* (Berlin, 1921), Bd. II.
22 *NIW*, May 22, 1992; Werner Röder and Herbert A. Strauss, eds., *Biographisches Handbuch der deutschsprachigen Emigration nach 1933–1945* (München, 1999), 442.
23 Tarik Cyril Amar, *The paradox of Ukrainian Lviv: A borderland city between stalinists, nazis, and nationalists* (Ithaca, 2015), 27.
24 *The history of the Jews from Bielsko-Biala* (Tel Aviv, 1987); Leo Baeck Institute, 6760.
25 John Klier and Shlomo Lambroza, eds., *Pogroms: Anti-Jewish violence in modern Russian history* (Cambridge, 1992); Stephen J. Zipperstein, *Pogrom: Kishinev and the tilt of history* (New York, 2018).
26 David G. Roskies, *The literature of destruction: Jewish responses to catastrophe* (Philadelphia, 1989).
27 Guttmann in: Hugo Claus et al., *Première* (Arnhem, 1958), 31–39.
28 On German terror, see: David Engel, *The Holocaust: The Third Reich and the Jews* (London and New York, 2013), 106.
29 Diethelm Blecking, 'Jews and sports in Poland before the Second World War,' in *Jews and the sporting life: Studies in contemporary Jewry XXIII*, ed. Ezra Mendelsohn (Oxford, 2008).
30 Jeannette R. Malkin, 'Introduction,' in *Jews and the making of modern German theatre*, eds. Jeannette R. Malkin and Freddie Rokem (Iowa City, 2010), 1–21, 11.
31 B&G, 'Anders dan anderen,' TV Show, VARA, May 1, 1962.
32 *Westerbork Girl*. Documentary, Steffy van den Oord, VPRO, 2007. *Westerbork Serenade*, play by Edwin de Vries and Sam de Vries, 2016.
33 B&G: Polygoon cinema news reel, week 52, December 24, 1945. The poem '*Achter de horizon*' is by Willem van Iependaal (translation: re).
34 *de Volkskrant*, September 1, 1969.
35 Rob de Vries's official debut was in 1938. UvA: Brvrir004, De Vries to Koenderink, June 1, 1947.
36 Eduard Necker Veterman, *Keizersgracht 763: Een blauwboek* (Amsterdam, 1946), 58–59, 82–83.
37 UvA: Brvriro66, lecture notes R. de Vries.
38 Based on *Westerbork Girl*, a conversation and telephone calls with Edwin de Vries, June 15, 2020, June 18, 2020.
39 Walter Benjamin, 'Excavation and memory,' in *Selected writings*, eds. Marcus Paul Bullock et al., vol. 2 (Cambridge, 2005), 576; Aleida Assmann, *Cultural memory and Western civilization: Functions, media, archives* (Cambridge, 2011), 150–154.
40 Piet Meeuse, 'Een systematische vergroting van het raadsel. Over Mulisch' "De Compositie van de Wereld",' *De Revisor* 8 (1987): 24–33; J.M. Coetzee, 'Harry

Mulisch, the discovery of heaven,' in *Stranger shores: Literary essays* (New York, 2001), 39–48.

41 Maurits Dekker and Albert Helman, *Vrij Volk: Herdenkingsstuk bij de bevrijding van ons land in mei 1945* (Amsterdam, 1945), premiere, June 6, 1945; *De Waarheid*, June 7, 1945.

42 A. Defresne, *De naamloozen van 1942. Tragi-comedie in vijf bedrijven* (Amsterdam, 1945); premiere, July 7, 1945.

43 *NIW*, March 22, 1946.

44 According to the director in 1946, www.albertvandalsum.nl (accessed January 3, 2021).

45 *NIW*, March 22, 1946; Maurits Dekker, *Afscheid. Een monoloog* (Amsterdam, 1946); premiere, February 28, 1946.

46 *NIW*, April 21, 1972; Mendel Kohansky, *The Hebrew theater; its first fifty years* (New York, 1969), 146–147; Theodore Bikel, *Theo: The autobiography of Theodore Bikel* (New York, 1994), 35.

47 *De ring en de kelim*: premiere, March 19, 1949; Luisa Treves, *Van achteren naar voren: Verzameld toneelwerk* (Amsterdam, 1989), 281–349; conversation, Felix Guttmann, June 26, 2020, Amsterdam.

48 UvA: Brgutt003, Guttmann to Treves, 1949; Brgutt004, Guttmann to De Meester jr., October 29, 1949; Brgutt005, Guttmann to De Meester Jr., December 2, 1949.

Figure 4 The dramatists Frances Goodrich and Albert Hackett and director Garson Kanin are shown around in the Secret Annex by Otto Frank, December 1954 (Maria Austria/MAI)

2 Under erasure

From diary to script

As Mr. Frank reads on, another voice joins in, as if coming from the air. It is Anne's voice.

–Act 1, Scene 1–

Adaptation

This is the opening scene of *The Diary of Anne Frank*. A man stumbles up the stairs to what looks like one dusty garret but actually splits up into a labyrinth of separate rooms. He picks up a glove from the floor, passes an overturned chair and puts on a scarf that he finds hanging on a hook. The carillon of the Westertoren strikes, we hear children's voices, then a barrel organ. The light is dim, the man continues and almost collapses. A young woman who, as we notice, is pregnant comes to his aid. She hands the man a bundle of papers and a short dialogue follows. The audience is introduced to Otto Frank, Miep Gies and the diary of Anne Frank.

The play's opening with Otto's ghostly return from the camps was perhaps the most drastic facet of the diary's stage adaptation. The scene turned the diary into a segment of a frame story that focused not only on life during wartime but also on postwar feelings of loss, giving spectators an opening to connect with the story and tap into their own memories. To these same spectators, Mr. Frank must have appeared bewildered when his reticent words didn't match the pull of objects scattered around in the room.

> I can't stay in Amsterdam, Miep. It has too many memories for me. Everywhere there's something. . . . The house we lived in . . . the school . . . that street organ playing out there.

Otto, meanwhile, picks up the glove – without explaining its appeal – and puts it in his rucksack, almost simultaneously ordering Miep to burn the

DOI: 10.4324/9781032034324-3

papers. 'Burn this?' she replies. It's the diary. Otto receives the notebook and starts reading, first without intonation:

> 'Monday, the sixth of July, nineteen forty-two . . .' Is it possible, Miep . . . Only three years.

Otto continues reading while Anne's voice takes over – 'as if coming from the air,' according to a stage direction. Sound, clothing, set design, props, movement and speech: all were called in to evoke a survivor's sense of alienation – out of time, out of place – and despair far removed from the joyful feelings conventionally associated with the liberation in the Netherlands. This made for an interesting shift in the dramatization of war, away from nationalism and martial heroism. The scene made the absent presence of Anne tangible, enhanced by mnemonic metaphors such as the transfer of the diary and the objects scattered across a dusty attic.

The opening scene is surprising given that it takes place after Anne's death and is therefore beyond the scope of the diary. Clearly, the relationship between the diary and the script as adaptation deserves further scrutiny. Anne began her diary on June 12, 1942, three weeks before the family went into hiding. It covers the entire period in hiding with the last entry dating from August 1, 1944, three days before the arrest – in fact, the diary is punctuated by blanks of the dates with no entry. Anne's papers were left on the floor when the families were taken away. The period after the arrest is therefore not part of the diary entries. However, the diary cannot only be seen as a direct reflection of the writer's experience and presence, at a specific, uniquely dated moment in time. We can imagine both the genocidal terror and postwar grief if we recognize allusions in Anne's writings that go beyond an unmediated presence. And if we see the making of a theatrical adaptation as a license to transform these allusions into a script that juggles with notions of presence and absence.

How did the playwrights operate, in scripting the contents of the diary? The opening scene already provides an important clue: they did so by emphatically presenting a memory play in which the diary acts as a shard to unlock the past and manifest Anne's precarious presence on stage.

Adaptation is a two-way street.[1] The script was derived from the diary but also came to affect the diary, yet the diary came on the scene well prepared. The practice of adapting novels and memoirs for the stage goes back two centuries.[2] Or further back, when not so much an explicit acknowledgment of an adaptation, but the literary strategy itself is central. The practice is now so common that reading a book can take place in anticipation of a future adaptation not unlike how Anne Frank anticipated her diary's future reading or recitation: '*it must seem quite funny if . . .*' The stage adaptation picked up on Anne's anticipatory and preparatory work by a series of radical interventions, erasures and additions. The diary provided an opening for this, such as when Anne mused about future treatments of her diary, or maybe she even laid the foundations.

Anne Frank – dramatist

Anne Frank wrote her notes first in the checkered diary she received on her 13th birthday and then in various available notebooks. At least one notebook with the entries from 1943 is believed to have been lost, two notebooks have survived. When she heard the call for diaries on the radio, March 1944, Anne had no intention of simply handing in her minutes but instead sought to have a complete manuscript ready. While diary keeping was a trend among female adolescents as far back as the nineteenth century, Anne's decision to re-edit her notes was remarkable and created something unique and meant to be somehow reiterated in public. The project was realized at a breathtaking pace, on colored loose pages of which 330 survived.[3] Or maybe it's safe to say that Anne laid the foundation for a project that never materialized.

Anne's editing was something of an adaptation with an audience in mind. In a way, the book publication as instigated by Otto Frank was another adaptation. Otto's actual return went at a different pace than suggested by the opening scene. Auschwitz was liberated on March 5, but it was not until June 3 before he was back in Amsterdam. It took another six weeks before Otto became certain of the fate of his daughters. When Miep Gies handed him the diaries, it would take another two months before he found the courage to start reading. The time had come to the end of September. Otto was overwhelmed by his daughter's 'indescribably exciting' diary.[4] He began to make transcriptions and translations that he read out loud to friends in Amsterdam and sent to his family in Basel. Later he received help.

When preparing for the play, Karl Guttmann entered into a correspondence with Otto to have him clarify some details. Otto explained that at the time he 'felt a strong urge to share the diary with intimate friends' as to talk about it. Paula Salomon-Lindberg who had known Anne very well was among these first readers, as she wrote Guttmann when he was working in Germany. She had to deal with her own loss, and she and Otto sought each other out for mutual support. Like Otto (who, as she wrote, had indeed been on a search in the annex for a keepsake '*an die seinen*'), she excused herself from visiting the play: '*Wir stehen diesem Stück zu nahe.*'[5] During this three-month period, Fall 1945, the idea for a publication arose.

It's often said that it was extremely difficult to find a publisher for the diary, but it's actually striking how quickly Otto succeeded in his venture.

After a recommendation in the newspaper *Het Parool*, April 1946, a publisher contacted Otto and in June a monthly magazine published an excerpt sandwiched between a scientific essay, an excerpt from a novel and some poetry. Not bad for a first-time author! June 25, 1947, *Het Achterhuis* was published in an edition of 3,000 copies.[6]

Otto's compilation was mainly based on Anne's revision. His editing consisted of selecting sections and omitting or putting back phrases that Anne had dealt with in her own revision. Selections aside, the most notable intervention on this point was the inclusion of pseudonyms that Anne had written on a loose sheet of paper. The list contained 13 names. The Van Pels family was nicknamed Van Daan, dentist Pfeffer became Dussel. The postwar editors did not include all names on the list, others were modified and some names not on the list were changed all the same or swapped for a random initial. Dussel was the only one with an obvious semantic importance. Dussel means duffer in German and so it was duffy Dussel who appeared in the publication – but not in the handwritten diaries – as Anne's Nemesis. All this was initiated by one of the editors with Otto's approval, making it odd that the name changes are still attributed to Anne without further explanation.[7] It was an act that, depending on the perspective, questions or strengthens Anne's authorship. It furthermore underscores her sense of role play.

There's a case to be made for nominating Anne Frank not only as the first editor of the diary but also as the first dramatist. To begin with, she was familiar with drama and fond of the glamour of film. Anne collected photos of movie stars and she and her BFF 'Jopie' (Jacqueline van Maarsen) went through every episode of *Cinema & Theater*, a magazine that devoted varying attention to film and theater.[8] Anne read much in the secret annex and her reading pattern changed, partly under pressure from the circumstances. At first she was lyrical about the young adult book writer Cissy van Marxveldt, whose books gave her the idea of writing in epistolary form. She then switched to non-fiction and adult literature.[9] Reading drama became part of Anne's cultural education. She began reading a series of plays by Theodor Körner, a popular nineteenth-century writer of light-hearted comedies. 'I think this man writes amusingly,' notes 13-year-old Anne announcing that Friedrich Hebbel is also on her menu. These classics from the rock-solid prewar German canon must have come straight from the sleeve of Mr. Frank. Not unlike Guttmann's canonical list of Friedrich Schiller, Heinrich Von Kleist, Franz Grillparzer and Hebbel.[10] One day Otto took Goethe's and Schiller's dramas 'out of the big bookcase' to read to Anne every night. 'We've already started with [Schiller's] *Don Carlos*' – staged at least twice by *Don Carlos* Guttmann, in Vienna and Rotterdam.[11] This was followed by *Maria Stuart* (the first play Guttmann directed in the Netherlands), *Die*

Jungfrau von Orleans and *Wilhelm Tell*. They also read *Nathan der Weise* by Gotthold Ephraim Lessing. Evidence for having read Shakespeare's *The Merchant of Venice* (staged by Guttmann in 1966) with Nathan's antitype Shylock is missing.

Theater was also something to do for herself from an early age. With Jopie – nicknamed after a character, Anne reenacted the stories of Van Marxveldt whose books were actually frequently adapted for the stage.[12] On her visits to the Swiss family, when she was still young, Anne played a lot with her cousin Buddy whom she encouraged to dress up and perform plays: 'She loved theater!' and so did Buddy, and while Anne was in hiding he had made his debut in a Lessing play.[13] In elementary school, she acted in a play. Her class at the Jewish Secondary staged a Greek play, 'something with Zeus and robes,' but by then Anne probably was already in hiding.[14]

In the annex, writing became a new mode for Anne to explore the boundaries of her personality. The diary letters assume the existence of a world outside the walls of Fort Annex as if she was still in contact with her friends. Pen pal Kitty was unaware of any war whatsoever, as she literally wrote on April 3, 1944. All of her writings could serve as personal explorations and inner conversations but with an outside readership in mind, fictitious for lack of a better term. The format of a correspondence arouses a mutual empathetic understanding between Anne and Kitty, and the reader becomes part of this. One early Dutch reviewer concluded Anne's diary might not be 'real' (*echt*) enough, not in the sense of being fake but in the way in which the writer was pursuing a rhetorical effect with a future audience in mind. The complaint substantiates the romantic conception of a diary as the direct reflection of the author's inner self. Anne's writing got in the way of her presence.[15]

Drama seeped into Anne's writing first by choice of words – Sinterklaas 1942 was her 'premiere' – and then by construing *Het Achterhuis* as a literary and dramatic construction. An example is the short story 'The Dentist' (December 8, 1942) in which Pfeffer took up his profession for the first time after his arrival.

> Today we had the most beautiful scene I've ever seen in this place. . . . Now the turmoil really began. Madam hit where she could. . . . Mister Pfeffer just stood there, hands on his hips and calmly overseeing the scene. The rest of the spectators laughed uncontrollably.[16]

Anne read the story out loud to the annexants![17] May 16, 1944, she wrote a theater dialogue consisting of 12 lines. Mrs. Van Pels made a defeatist remark about the German defenses and her husband responded. After some bickering, Mr. Van Pels called his wife to shut up. *End of Act 1*.

Anne evoked the typical hiding situation in which everyone must take the other into account: keep the truce, stay in line, pretend, feign, act. Living together was an ordeal and acting a survival strategy. 'It is mighty difficult to be on such model behavior with people you can't stand, especially when you don't mean a word of it. But I really do see that I'm all better off by shamming a bit.'[18] These notes are reminiscent of the dramaturgical perspective of sociologist Erving Goffman who argued that everyday social behavior can best be understood by introducing stage metaphors such as front and backstage.[19] In 'normal life' – as Anne called it – it's already difficult to safeguard the boundaries of public and private and the thresholds of shame and loss of face. In hiding it was sheer impossible to keep up appearances. All deep-seated feelings and daily behavior had to be redefined. The diary offered readers a sometimes painful glimpse into the private sphere. Yet recalling back- and frontstage also functioned as a rhetorical device, enticing the reader with the promise of a backstage view. Anne, the backstage girl, describes an intimate moment when she and Margot agreed to read a fragment from each other's diary while nosy Mrs. Van Pels was ostentatiously turned away.[20] All this makes it more appropriate to make quotes on stage sound as whispered aside, ad spectatores at most.

Anne's dramaturgical exploration culminates in the last diary entry. She famously recalled the image of herself as 'a little bundle of contradictions' and then explained herself further with the drama metaphors within reach.

> Certainly, I'm a giddy clown for one afternoon, but then everyone's had enough of me for another month. Really, it's exactly like a romance film for deep thinkers, simply a diversion, an entertaining interlude. . . . Sometimes, if I really compel the good Anne to take the stage for a quarter of an hour and she has to speak, she just shrivels up like a touch-me-not. . . . If I'm quiet and serious, everyone thinks it's a new comedy.[21]

In writing her diary, Anne delineated a self in relation to a world inside and outside of the annex, but she nor the reader can find solid ground. Her editorial work included mining her memory, which, in fact, is true of all of her writing. While maintaining the sequence of dates and inserting entries as befits the genre, she flipped back, reread, recalled her life from the past, possibly followed by retrospectively rewriting entries and dismissing some of her earlier entries as dated. Striking is the edited entry, dated January 2, 1944, but jotted down in the summer of that same year.

> I tried to understand the Anne of last year and make apologies for her. . . . I hid inside myself, only considered myself and calmly wrote down all my joy, jest and sorrow. This diary has value to me, because

> it has become a book of memoirs in many places but on a good many pages I could certainly put 'past and done with.'[22]

Anne Frank had two long 'contemplative years' – *denkjaren* – in the secret annex, as she wrote when she turned 15.[23] Writing became a quest for a form that could most adequately express her thoughts and imaginations. That quest – her many musings – yielded a diary in the format of a pen pal correspondence, borrowed from a youth novel, while the results of Anne's unfinished revisions yielded a mixture of diary, scrapbook and memoirs, hinting at a detective and perhaps working toward an amusing ('funny') history book.

All in all, the published diary seems less straightforward in terms of authorship and genre. Retroactively, the book publication was 'the original' of the stage adaptation, but where did that leave the handwritten diaries or Otto's editing? Then there are the genre citations that shaped Anne's writings. Moreover, in re-editing her diary, dates no longer referred to the proper dates of writing. Anne rewrote *as if* she were writing her daily entries. Add to this how the older Anne no longer fully identified with the writings of her former self. She felt absent in real life and present in her writings. But not always.

It can be concluded that the 1986 critical edition in which the versions were juxtaposed did not reveal so much an original Anne or a core meaning. Instead, readers were made aware of the need to focus on Anne's writing as a continuous activity – which is actually an ongoing theme in the diary. This inference isn't remarkable in itself, but it is quite explosive when it comes to Anne Frank: the question of authorship even gave rise to the authentication research underlying the critical edition. I think it is nevertheless crucial to accentuate Anne's writing, not only as a noun but also as a verb. This also explains how for more than 30 years her diary became involved in a series of readings, recitations and rewrites: strategies that necessarily prioritize certain traces while erasing others or giving some characters a voice while silencing others.

The call on Radio Oranje was meant to collect diaries as a form of archiving the German occupation. Anne instead had a future audience in mind. A moving moment arrives when the reader reaches the last page of the diary, August 1, three days before the arrest. Arguably, there's a second final entry, March 29, 1944. This is the last edited entry. For all we know, Anne continued to edit her previous entries after August 1, making March 29 the very last page she wrote. First Anne wrote her lines on 'future's yesterday'

> But seriously now, ten years after the war it must seem quite funny if it were told how we lived here as Jews, what we ate and what we were talking about.

Figure 5 Merwede Square, 1935, a few years after it was completed. From 1933, the Frank family lived at 37, that is the portico on the right, opposite the pushcart (postcard, artist unknown, Stadsarchief Amsterdam)

A future retelling was thus inscribed in the diary. Anne used the Dutch indefinite pronoun *men* (*vertelt*). Sometime later, in her editing, she copied the sentence but then erased one word. She now chose the pronoun *we*: *wij vertellen*, we tell.

> But seriously now, ten years after the war it must seem quite funny if we were to tell how we lived here as Jews, what we ate and what we were talking about.

It was through the still visible erasure that Anne Frank presented herself as a writer while it also expressed the fate that befell her. Anne told a future audience that this then is her telling us about life in the annex but in the end it were told.

A visit to the secret annex

Otto's arrival and state of confusion would hand the Hacketts their opening scene. The core was already in a June 1954 version of the script, but a visit to Amsterdam will have contributed to the detailing of the scene. At the time, the annex still exuded the same atmosphere they wanted to evoke in the cinematic opening scene: an abandoned and dusty space where the residents had left headlong, where the ghosts of the past roamed and where no one had dared since to set foot. Although the latter was not entirely correct.

The visit sowed the seed for the Dutch production, but it is especially interesting because of the intentions and experiences of the US team. On their visit, they came to relive and re-experience the sites from the diary, recalling Anne's writings and retracing her steps. It is remarkable how closely the diary became linked to all kinds of sites. The diary is connected to the hiding place but also to a number of other places. The Hacketts have been instrumental in citing these sites.

The Hacketts and Kanin arrived in Amsterdam on December 6, 1954.[24] With some satisfaction, they settled in the Amstel hotel with a view of the river after which the posh hotel was named. Exactly a year before, the couple had been commissioned to convert *The Diary of a Young Girl* into a play. As of January 1954, they had committed themselves to writing a satisfactory script. After a number of versions, some breakdowns ('Terrible emotional impact. I cry all the time,' as Goodrich wrote in her 'Diary of The Diary of Anne Frank.') and obtaining advice from various specialists, the script was accepted. They had not yet met Kanin nor visited Amsterdam. So more amendments would follow.[25]

It had been Kanin's suggestion to travel to Amsterdam to gain inspiration for the stage design and the scenography. He was a successful jack-of-all-trades in the dramatic arts, writing and directing for theater and film, which must have made it easier for him to step in at this stage. At least, since Kanin sent a 17-page list of revisions before the three even met, we can presume that lack of confidence was not one of his traits. If it were up to him, the script was still under construction and the Hacketts did not seem to object to that assessment. Their mood could not be ruined, not yet at least.

Kanin's suggestion to study 'details of background, national characteristics, history, architecture, dress, and food' seemed like an ethnographic expedition. In that case, it would have been smarter to arrive a day earlier, that is, on the day that *Sinterklaas* is celebrated – as happened in the secret annex in 1942 and 1943. Otto Frank knew as he had left them gifts in the hotel. Together they visited the prewar home of the Frank family at 37 Merwede Square and the primary school, both situated in the Rivierenbuurt – a neighborhood in which all streets were named after rivers from the Low Countries. They also went by ice cream parlor Oasis that was still 'allowed for Jews,' as Anne wrote in her diary, and one assumes they took a peek at the store where Anne's diary was bought as one of the gifts for her 13th birthday. These were the locations in the small world of a girl who attended primary school. Anne's world had however already expanded because of her attending high school, which became the enforced segregated 'Jewish' Lyceum, a Public Secondary on the other side of the Amstel River and close to the hotel. It is referenced early on in the play as Peter and Anne discuss their common school past. The transfer of nearly 500 schoolchildren to the Jewish Secondary brought middle-class children like Anne into contact with the 'miserable and shabby' atmosphere of the Jewish quarter, as recalled by a surviving classmate.[26] Before the war, the Rivierenbuurt was a new neighborhood for the better-off middle class, including many Jewish families. Herbert Nelson lived at 19 and 23 Merwede Square, where he secretly organized theater – and that included Enny Mols.[27] The square opened onto the wide Amstel Avenue where Fritz Pfeffer had his dental practice and Jan and Annie Romein came to live, the two historians who gave the diary a definitive publicity push in April 1946.

The next stop was the secret annex. The trio wished to trace the route the Frank family had followed on their way to 263 Prinsengracht on July 6, 1942, in the pouring rain. It is referenced early on in the play when the Frank family is late on their first appointment. Mr. Van Daan reassures his wife and their son Peter they 'have two miles to walk.' In his prompt book, Karl Guttmann found it worth noting to remind the actors that on their first stage entrance, they had just walked exhaustively through the rain for 45 minutes.

A visit to the hiding place made sense, but it would be an exaggeration to say that it was inescapable. First of all, the 'front house' – as opposed to the 'hind house' or annex – was still in operation to trade herbs and pectin, a substance to prepare jam; actually it had never ceased to function. Otto Frank was forced, like all Jewish entrepreneurs to turn ownership over to a 'non-Jew.' Nevertheless, he had tried to continue running the company, almost literally, from behind the scenes. In 1954, the structure was nominated for demolition. The terrifying specter of modernization that had been responsible for clearing so many tattered city centers also haunted Amsterdam. In particular, the former Jewish quarter would be at the receiving end from the late 1950s, without much respect for the memories and feelings of survivors. The canal houses were not protected against demolition either. The property on the Prinsengracht had not yet been transformed into a monument where day after day the rows of visitors turn the corner. On the last day of the trio's visit, one newspaper responded to the news of the demolition with a printed shrug of the shoulders: 'Well then, at least the book endures.'[28] The play would change all of this.

In 1954, there was an occasional knock on the door followed by a tour of the locations in the diary. Especially one of the helpers, Johannes Kleiman, took on this role as a provisional guide. In fact, that was what happened when the trio arrived at the premises. It must have been quite busy on the narrow steep steps and tight spaces: Frank, Goodrich, Hackett, Kanin and Kleiman. Add to this two photographers: Maria Austria and her colleague and husband Henk Jonker. Kanin wanted to record as many of his findings as possible so that the sound and set designers could get to work. In the photos of Maria Austria, you see him diligently taking notes while the writers listen to Otto's explanation with interest, yet more as if they were on a regular touristic excursion – as they also rounded off their stay with a visit to the Rijksmuseum.[29]

Photographer Maria Austria captured the annex so that the set could be built on that base. The presence of Austria leads us directly to Rob as he seems to have recommended her to Otto, perhaps through an intermediary. The photographer had grown up as Maria Oestreicher in the German-speaking world of the Austro-Habsburg empire that was nearing its end. In the middle of her studies, she fled from Vienna to the Netherlands and built up a practice as photographer. Austria and De Vries had joined the resistance and this laid the foundation for a lifelong friendship.[30]

Austria also had a history in common with Karl as they both had lived in Vienna in the same prewar years. As with Rob, Austria would be responsible for a few family photos of the Guttmann family.[31] Finally, the photographer seems to have developed a bond with Otto that morning. Before the war, Austria lived a few numbers from the Frank family on Merwede Square – but there is no evidence of an encounter at the time. Austria's biographer stresses how relaxed Otto appears in the photos that day. At one point, the photographer took him aside and asked him to roll up his sleeve so that she could photograph his Auschwitz tattoo. Austria took care of two orphaned nieces. De Vries suggested that one of the two play the part of Anne. Austria thought it was a bad idea because reality and fiction would mix too much.[32]

All in all, it was a peculiar gathering of people who were connected in different ways and who had assembled that day around 15-year-old Anne's miraculously preserved diary. It was depressing and moving at the same time. Frances Goodrich was baffled by the tight spaces, Kanin was surprised to see a cutout glamourous photo of Ginger Rogers on the wall of Anne's room. The publicity photo was made for *Tom Dick and Harry*, a movie he directed in 1941. How had that picture ended up there, he wondered. There was an advertising photo of Maria Austria on the same wall. Moving about quietly, Kanin became obsessed, as he noted in his memoirs, 'by the shuddering notion that we, not the missing ones, were the ghosts.' And, as if that wasn't uncanny enough, he is said to have spent the night in the secret annex, 'trying to imagine the experience of its inhabitants,' including the effect of the outdoor noise. Did he sleep there with a December night temperature below zero degrees Celsius or was he there just for an hour or so to soak up the atmosphere? Otto was unable to cope with the memories brought back from the many conversations with the visitors. After the guests had left, Mr. Cold Fish, as Kanin called Otto, collapsed and remained off the map for a few days.[33]

The Hacketts weren't the first to take a walk through memory lane. Post-war memorial activities often took this form (more on walking in Chapter 5), naming and mourning the dead of the ruined Jewish quarter. In their case, there was the detour of the diary – which probably also prevented them from visiting the old Jewish neighborhood. Their visit would inform the script, as a supplement to the diary, and directly determined the soundscape and the decor.

A visit to the Institute for War Documentation was planned for the next day, two canals further at 474 Herengracht. Here the diary collection was deposited that Minister Bolkestein had asked for via Radio Oranje. This visit functioned as an authorization of the dramatists' adaptation. As if Anne's diary needed an addition and outside confirmation, so as director Kanin could declare on the last day in Amsterdam that 'not a spark of fantasy had been added.' The three visited Loe de Jong, the director whose assignment was to write a history of the German occupation. May 1940, De Jong managed to flee to England. His parents and twin brother were killed. At the time of the Hacketts' visit, he was working, among other things, on a widely read article on Anne Frank for the Reader's Digest.[34] De Jong read the script for errors. Hackett publicly lauded the historian: 'If numbers are mentioned in any of the dialogues, they are certainly the undeniable historical truth!'[35] De Jong's Bureau also sent the Americans a copy of the yellow badge. A few years later, the historian tried his hands on a screenplay himself. *The Silent Raid* (*De Overval*, dir. Paul Rotha, 1962) was a feature film about a prison outbreak during the war with Rob de Vries in an heroic lead.

Just before their departure, the Hacketts had one last lunch with Otto Frank and an interview with *Het Parool*. Rob de Vries had asked the journalist to check about an option on the play. The Hacketts returned to London on December 11, followed by a Christmas holiday in Paris: both were 'emotionally destroyed.'[36] January 1955, the playwrights submitted their tentative final script that gave a new spin to the diary. The first test performance was scheduled for February, but the producer unexpectedly decided to postpone the premiere until the fall. Much to the horror of the Hacketts.

From the air

The American writer Meyer Levin was probably the first to see the theatrical possibilities after reading the diary in a French translation. Levin had some reason to identify with Anne: as a Jewish journalist, he had had a transformative experience when he came face to face with the horror of liberated Bergen-Belsen. He pitched his idea for an adaptation and, after some hesitation, Otto agreed. The project went astray when American producers got involved. Levin's script was rejected, even after several rewrites, and the producers went looking for a dramatist with a different take and more prestige.[37] Levin saw the play as a moment of mourning and an opportunity to revive postwar Judaism. The producers were looking for a less morose take.

The producers' search led to a writing couple that were known for their comedy. Frances Goodrich and Alfred Hackett had made their mark in the world of Hollywood and Broadway. Their dialogues were appreciated for their homely bickering atmosphere, witty and full of quips. Very modern, according to the critics.[38] It was this light touch that earned them the assignment, one that recalled their successful drama. Broadway theater, as the producer continued to hammer home, demanded an easily digestible play, sad and uplifting at the same time: a play that circumvents the unavoidable spoiler-alert.

The tag of adaptation was part of a commercial strategy and meant to tap in to new audiences. Production was a precarious endeavor, however, and the US team was worried the show would turn out a flop. The lengthy tinkering with the script can be explained in this way as it might account for the legal issues. Levin's rejected script was banned from performing, and the Hacketts script attained an almost untouchable status. It's ironic that at the time of the 1986 critical edition, the diary that should be solid as an archival item turned out to be more playful than the fossilized script.

The final script – the black-covered typescript that was sent to Karl Guttmann, August 1956 – consisted of ten scenes spread over two Acts.

ACT 1

Scene 1: Otto returns, 1945
Scene 2: The two families meet, 1942
Scene 3: Daily life and Dussel's arrival
Scene 4: Anne's nightmare
Scene 5: Hanukkah and burglary

ACT 2

Scene 6: Bickering about the New Year's cake, 1944
Scene 7: The rendezvous of Anne and Peter
Scene 8: The theft of bread and the invasion
Scene 9: Anne's maxim and the arrest
Scene 10: Otto's and Anne's final words, 1945

Aside from the prelude and the epilogue, the scenes cover the actual period of two years in hiding. The first Act consists of an *exposition*: a round of introductions of the two families, the rules to live by and a taste of Anne's jumpy character. After this, the *intrigue* could be rolled out: against the threat of war and persecution, Anne tries to give meaning to her life as a maturing teenager, while the others with the greatest effort try to keep the peace. This leads to a provisional *climax* in the last scene before the break, a drawn-out celebration of Hanukkah that is disturbed by a burglary. After the intermission, the love between Anne and Peter takes center stage and Anne manages to translate her experiences into a moral message with a broader scope: 'I still believe, in spite of everything, that people are really good at heart.' The *resolution* comes with the arrest and an epilogue on the fate of the eight annexants. The play finally ends with an *apotheosis* as when Anne's voice is heard one last time and in which she once more expresses her trust that people are essentially good at heart.

The play is well organized. Acts 1 and 2 are each other's complement. In Act 1, Anne and Peter bicker, but the community is more or less intact (as symbolized in Hanukkah); in Act 2, Anne and Peter grow closer, but the community gradually falls apart (mainly because of the two *antagonists* that have to bear the burden of their fair share of the seven deadly sins: supercilious outsider Dussel and gluttonous thief Van Daan). The fictional theft was introduced at the very last minute out of concern that the play would collapse in Act 2.[39]

The script reflects the precariousness of Anne's status, being absent yet bearing testimony through the presence of her diary. The Hacketts looked for theatrical ways to meet these insights. In the opening scene, the audience is led into the past via the recitation of the diary. This link between Anne, diary and annex was reinforced by an artifice. Anne Frank was one of many diarists during WWII. Some carried on their writing from before the occupation and others saw the war as a significant time to start a diary. The Hacketts decided to situate the gift of the diary in the annex. They also made it appear that some annexants only got to know each other in the annex. This act of synchronizing time and place corrected the diary, as it were and contributed to a stronger symbolic connection between Anne, annex and diary. As if her life was seamlessly connected with the annex and as if she had never left the room and may in fact appear at any moment.

Another device was the use of a voice-over. In the intermissions, Anne's voice would recite quotations from her diary as if from the air. This provided continuity during set arrangements and informed the audience about the passage of time. The voice-over authenticated the play and turned Anne into a theatrical ghost. It was as if Kanin wanted to reiterate his encounter with Anne's presence in the secret annex – 'as if the living were the ghosts' – onstage. The latter becomes particularly clear when Anne is allowed to utter her aphorism 'as if from the air' in the last post-war scene. The play is uncanny to the end! It is funny to think the dramatic construction follows and is a reversal of *Hamlet*. There it's Hamlet's father who calls his son to avenge his death, *Murder most foul*, here it's the daughter who calls her father to spread the word of love since in spite of everything 'people are really good at heart.' Whereas Anne's life and work were fractured, the propitious citation was meant to encompass an aphoristic whole.

The aphorism was derived from an entry (July 15, 1944) in which Anne displays a more ambiguous outlook. First she shelved her 'absurd' ideals, picturing a world that 'turns into a wilderness. . . . I hear the ever-approaching thunder, which will destroy us too.'[40] The Hacketts deleted these lines and opted here for a liberal upbeat reading that ignored Anne's more disquieting thoughts: 'In spite of everything I still believe that people are really good at heart.' They distilled a thoughtful message from Anne's writing turning thinking into Thought. The message was in accordance with the universalization the dramatists and Otto were after.[41] And to some degree they were right. The diary was unique as the dated account of one Jewish adolescent in hiding, but its meaning was hardly solid. For example, in the first Dutch reviews the diary was recommended more because of the recognizable parent–child entanglements than as an account of the persecution. Just as the diary was generic as one of almost 2,000 'war diaries,' archived by De Jong's Institute. Anne's fate was like all victims labeled as members of a community destined to be erased from this world. There was, however, a catch.

The Hacketts injected the play with a forward-looking ideology, a utopian call to put aside the burden of the past and look to an open future, thanks to a Christian understanding of exculpation and salvation. Instead, Anne inscribed her fate in a Jewish persecution history. At least that's one forceful way the diary can be read. The credibility of the Hacketts' reading depended on the aphorism and a second quotation that were brought together in one clause, pronounced by Anne in a dialogue with Peter: 'We're not the only people that've had to suffer. There've always been people that've had to . . . sometimes one race . . . sometimes another.' The diary entry of April 11, 1944, suggests the exact opposite:

> Who has inflicted this upon us? Who has made us Jews different to all other people? . . . But it will be God, too, who will raise us up again. If we bear all this suffering . . . then Jews, instead of being doomed, will be held up as an example.

Gone in the script was Anne's searching identification with Judaism, but the intervention did tie in with her view of a future in which Jews 'will be held up as an example.'

It makes sense to place the script in the early stages of Holocaust consciousness insofar as it attests to a typically generalizing vocabulary to express the Shoah, erasing the close relationship between persecution and Judaism. However, such reasoning leaves little room for idiosyncratic understandings by worldwide casts and their audiences that would take on the play. For present purposes, it is more constructive to try to grasp the layered theatrical handling of the diary as more than a collection of flaws. Just as the diary's meaning is deferred, so is that of the script.

Notes

1 Robert Stam, 'Beyond fidelity: The dialogics of adaptation,' in *Film adaptation*, ed. James Naremore (New Brunswick, 2000), 54–76.
2 Glenn Jellenik, 'On the origins of adaptation, as such: The birth of a simple abstraction,' in *The Oxford handbook of adaptation studies*, ed. Thomas Leitch (Oxford, 2017), 36–52.
3 Suzanne L. Bunkers, 'The complicated publication history of the Diaries of Anne Frank,' in *The diary: The epic of everyday life*, eds. Batsheva Ben-Amos and Dan Ben-Amos (Bloomington, 2020), 147–162.
4 Caroll Ann Lee, *The hidden life of Otto Frank: The biography* (New York, 2003), 196.
5 KG: a torn page of a notepad; letter Frank to Guttmann (no addressee and date) and Paula Lindberg to Guttmann, January 21, 1957. Lindberg's stepdaughter was the painter Charlotte Salomon (1917–1943).
6 Jan Romein, 'Kinderstem,' *Het Parool*, April 3, 1946; Lisa Kuitert, 'De uitgave van Het Achterhuis van Anne Frank,' *De Boekenwereld* 24 (2007–2008): 18–27.
7 For example, in David Barnouw, *The phenomenon of Anne Frank* (Bloomington, 2018), 36. For clarifications regarding the list, I thank Gertjan Broek, e-mail, October 29, 2019.
8 Frank, October 18, 1942; January 28, 1944 (A).
9 Ton J. Broos, 'De boekenplank van Anne Frank,' *Colloqium Neerlandicum* 15 (2003): 71–82.
10 Frank, October 18, 1942 (A).
11 Frank, October 29, 1942 (B); nickname in: KG: telegram for Guttmann, 1957.
12 Monica Soeting, 'De deemoed voorbij. Cissy van Marxveldt en haar rebellenclub,' *De Parelduiker* 13 (2008): 23–27.
13 *NOS Anne Frank 80 Jaar*. NPO TV show, June 12, 2009, www.npostart.nl/nos-anne-frank-80-jaar/POMS_S_NOS_104952; Frank, June 30, 1944 (A).
14 Dienke Hondius, *Absent: Herinneringen aan het Joods Lyceum Amsterdam, 1941–1943* (Amsterdam, 2001), 121.
15 'Over echte dagboeken gesproken,' *De Nederlander*, September 24, 1947.
16 Anne Frank, 'De tandarts,' in *Verhaaltjes, en gebeurtenissen uit het achterhuis*, ed. Joke Kniesmeijer (Amsterdam, 1986).

17 Otto Frank in *Meine Tochter, Anne Frank*, Docu-drama, direction Raymond Ley, 2015.
18 Frank, July 11, 1943 (B).
19 Erving Goffman, *The presentation of self in everyday life* (New York, 1959).
20 It is believed Margot's diary has gone missing.
21 Frank, August 1, 1944 (A).
22 Frank, January 2, 1944 (B).
23 Frank, June 13, 1944 (A).
24 Frances Goodrich, 'Diary of the "the diary of Anne Frank",' *The New York Times*, September 30, 1956; David L. Goodrich, *The real Nick and Nora: Frances Goodrich and Albert Hackett, writers of stage and screen classics* (Carbondale, IL, 2004), 213*ff*; Garson Kanin, *Hollywood: Stars and starlets, tycoons and flesh-peddlers, moviemakers and moneymakers, frauds and geniuses, hopefuls and has-beens, great lovers and sex symbols* (New York, 1967), 300.
25 The Hacketts and Kanin looked for rabbinic expertise and took advice from people in the United States who had escaped the persecution. Kanin in *Het Vaderland*, August 19, 1955, and Goodrich, 'Diary.'
26 Hondius, *Absent*, 105–106.
27 For the local history of Nelson pere and fils, see: Rian Verhoeven, *Anne Frank was niet alleen: Het Merwedeplein 1933–1945* (Amsterdam, 2019).
28 *De Tijd*, December 11, 1954.
29 Photography in MAI: File Maria Austria D1–12, 'Achterhuis Anne Frank.'
30 Conversation with Edwin de Vries, June 17, 2020.
31 E-mail, Felix Guttmann, August 21, 2020.
32 Martien Frijns, *Maria Austria: Fotografe* (Enschede, 2018), 728 and e-mails, June 23–24, 2020.
33 Kanin, *Hollywood*, 300.
34 Boudewijn Smits, *Loe de Jong 1914–2005: Historicus met een missie*. PhD thesis, Groningen, 2014 and e-mail, June 20, 2020; Loe de Jong, 'Anne Frank en haar dagboek,' *Het beste uit Reader's Digest* 1, 1 (October 1957).
35 *De Telegraaf*, September 14, 1955.
36 Goodrich, *The Real Nick and Nora*, 215–217; *Het Parool*, December 11, 1954.
37 Whether the Hacketts had taken note of Levin's script would become the subject of a lawsuit. See for this and further literature: Francine Prose, *Anne Frank: The book, the life, the afterlife* (New York, 2010); Lawrence Graver, *An obsession with Anne Frank: Meyer Levin and the "diary"* (Berkeley and Los Angeles, 1995).
38 Julie Berkobien, 'Frances Goodrich and Alfred Hackett: The most beloved couple in Hollywood,' in *When women wrote Hollywood: Essays on female screenwriters in the early film industry*, ed. Rosanne Welch (Jefferson, 2018), 140–149, 143.
39 The 'anti-climax' in Act 2 was mentioned in the Dutch press: *Leeuwarder Courant*, September 16, 1955. Anne mentions that both Pfeffer and Van Pels withheld food (not included in the C version): Frank, May 1 and September 29, 1943 (B).
40 Frank, May 15, 1944 (C).
41 Judith E. Doneson, 'The Americanization of Anne Frank's diary,' *Holocaust and Genocide Studies* 2, 1 (1987): 149–160.

Figure 6 The Hanukkah scene on set, November 1956 (Maria Austria/MAI)

3 A Holocaust performative

From script to play

[A] play about genuine people who had only recently died. Was that even appropriate?

–Anne-Marie Heyligers, stage actress

Survivors' ardor

The Netherlands was one of the first countries to apply for the performing rights of *The Diary of Anne Frank* and Otto Frank, with commonsense logic, was not in the least surprised, 'because it takes place in the Netherlands after all.' But early interest was above all due to the strong motivation of Rob de Vries who saw in the play an excellent opportunity to address the drama of war and spread the play's message to the far corners of the nation. The play was 'utterly important' and 'captured the spirit of the diary so well that it only could arouse admiration.' Attending a future performance would clearly have to be more than a fun night out: 'People want to forget at all costs and not to be reminded. In fact, they dread their memory and a certain sense of guilt surely has something to do with that,' as Rob professed while trying to convince an actress to take on the role of Edith Frank. 'I believe one of my most important duties is to blow the whistle at least once a year . . . and I'll do everything I can to be heard.' Drama was to provide society with the material to strengthen its moral fiber and the 'hugely important' play would be its vessel, a clarion call, 'fulfilling the purpose to just the right degree.'[1] Rob believed strongly in the capacity of theater to disrupt, to make the past extant and bring about a specter and a sentiment beyond the properties of the diary. Anne on stage would open the door to an uncomfortable past.

It was still a long way to go though. First the US team would sent the play signed, sealed and delivered as if it only took one flawless repeat, but that didn't take local circumstances, including fierce opposition, into account.

DOI: 10.4324/9781032034324-4

Theater would transform the horrible and incomparable into something conventional, an exercise in repetition, stage drama. Rob and Karl would have to pull out all the stops to meet the critical voices and give the play its subjective signature in their treatment of the script.

De Vries's allusions to the persecution were consistent with the profile of the Shoah in the public sphere. For a long time 'the war,' from which people 'had not come back,' was the common euphemism. Heleen Pimentel, the actress who declined Rob's role offer, spoke of her 'long vacation' in Westerbork and Terezin.[2] In many more instances, survivors remained silent, unwilling to speak or unable to find the proper words. Jules Croiset, who took on the role of Peter, called his father 'one of the notoriously silent Jews' with 'a tremendous sense of guilt for surviving the war carefree.' However, actor Max Croiset did write aphoristic lines of poetry, like in a dated reading of names – acknowledging an absence – from the collection *6 000 000*.[3]

1954

Louis Cohen
his wife
their children
barber Pruim
my little cousin Arie
the actor Van Praag

I have not seen them
since forty-two

Silence came in various forms. There was an absence of speech, there were remarks and allusions, as a word to the wise, and there were those that never stopped talking, at least in private. Memory was embodied yet not always enunciated. Rob was no doubt talking about the genocide, the current habitus of which he associated with feelings of guilt and fear – of being confronted with one's own memories. Resentment, mixed with a desire for closure, could very well be projected on the surviving European Jews as ubiquitous signs of a past to be forgotten as soon as possible. Yet there were also feelings of unease among survivors, and some of them made themselves heard after the American premiere. That prompted Otto to slow things down. Maybe the country wasn't ready to convert disquieting traces into a conventional cultural form like drama.

The first sign of contact was the Hacketts' visit to Amsterdam, but it is likely that Rob de Vries was keen to secure the rights from the first announcement of the upcoming dramatization – December 1953. He must have taken note of the press release with a mixture of interest and annoyance – as also later when he complained that the feature film should have been in Dutch hands.[4]

The structure of the Dutch theatrical field influenced the production of the play in that it handed the ensemble a monopoly but also a bigger responsibility. Just after the war, the country held four major subsidized theater companies based in each of the four major cities. Due to a new cultural policy – bring drama to the masses – this would gradually increase, but the general belief was that the small country could not handle much more if the ensembles were to remain viable. Companies fished in the same pond, looking for scripts for which they claimed exclusive performing rights. When after the war the unusual situation arose that *Death of a Salesman* was performed simultaneously by two ensembles (due to the lack of legal agreements with the United States), the critics were intrigued but the managers annoyed. The right of exclusivity only was abolished in the late 1960s. So for now there would be one production, one stage Anne and one single national conversation about the production. In Sweden, thanks to a commercial agent with American connections, five shows were up and running within a few months.[5] Germany took this to a new level with seven productions premiering in seven different cities on October 1, 1956.

A successful staging would not be unwelcome for De Vries in his new position as ensemble manager. Located in the eastern town of Arnhem and founded as part of the incipient policy of cultural dissemination, ensemble Theater had just passed its 25th performance at the time of the 1953 press release. Rob got a lot on his plate. He had to build a theater culture almost from scratch, find the actors who were willing to live 'in the boonies,' find suitable repertoire, maintain contacts with state and local officials, win subsidies, reach out to the youth and, last but not least, act.[6]

Who better suited than Rob to produce the play of which he hoped to convince Otto? In the week of the US premiere, Rob contacted Otto. First he tried to seduce Otto with his past. The play must be in the hands of 'someone who experienced the war most profoundly, especially in the Netherlands, where people will understand the events better than anywhere else in the world.' In his words, Rob seemed to evoke the emerging figure of a survivor with access to more authentic knowledge and moral rights. That was not a tactic as obvious as it now seems because the contours of the survivor were still in flux.[7] By introducing Otto as a returnee from the camps, the play in fact intervened amid a wealth of various associations to pin down the shape of victim and survivor: as Jewish/non-Jewish, as having been through a camp experience or having sheltered in a hideout as well as further aligning connotations: experiencing loss, grieving, being morally righteous, whose voice should be heard, having access to more authentic knowledge or experience, being too emotional or claiming a special status, having others fend for them in the war, etc. To be fair, Rob submitted his antecedents because he had been informed of Otto's wish to assess the moral weight of candidate theater practitioners. Karl Guttmann would put it as a sign of artistic approval for someone to get past Otto's veto.[8]

The play put the destruction of the Jews performatively on the map; the composition of the cast and the production of the play did not precede this but were in fact part of the memory work. Since New York, there was concern about the involvement of actors with a turbid war past. In the Netherlands, this affected actors that had continued working during the occupation. In order to do so, they first had to accept the segregation policies in October 1941 and then a few months later join the umbrella organization that the Nazis established to exclude 'Jews' and 'Jewish culture.' Some theater practitioners continued working out of ideological beliefs, many did so for other reasons: pragmatism, out of fear or to take care of vulnerable significant others. Harry Mulisch would publish a novel, *Last Call* (*Hoogste tijd*, 1985), that explored the theme: an elderly stage actor with a turbid past is rediscovered by a troupe of young actors for a part in *The Tempest*. That cannot end well. But there was a real-life example. The Austrian actress Gusti Huber, who took on the role of Edith Frank in New York, was targeted for her appointment with the Viennese Burgtheater after the Anschluss when Vienna had become a 'City without Jews.' The New York program notes suggested her career was 'abruptly terminated when the Germans overran Austria,' whereas in fact she had continued acting. During a press conference, Huber confessed she had performed in The Hague in 1942 and although she was 'deeply unhappy' at the time, she 'could not tell the frosty Dutch "we" were "anti" too.'[9]

But would a Dutch cast fare better? Perhaps it was better to set up a purified ad hoc cast, just as in 1945. De Vries instead went to bat for his own ensemble. 'As a Jew I went into hiding, worked "in the illegality" and was arrested. . . . After a year and a half in prisons and concentration camps, I fled. After the war, I was decorated by President Eisenhower.' If it didn't sound too flippant, it was like a bloated resume, using his underground activities to gain the upper hand. Historian Loe de Jong wrote an additional letter of recommendation. Given his heroic past, De Vries was 'the obvious choice.'[10] Otto Frank seemed convinced, but why then was everything going so slowly and when did that script actually come his way?[11]

Shortly after the New York premiere, the first Dutch reactions seeped in from diplomats, theater agents and also one helper, Mr. Kugler, who had moved to Canada after the war. Dutch readers could marvel at the intense Broadway atmosphere in which theater was a matter of life and death and spectators went to great lengths to get hold of tickets. But Anne Frank onstage, seriously? In Holland? Could such a show be staged in a country where thousands have been deported and many more watched others be deported? 'Yes of course you can and yes of course you should!' as the foreign correspondent called out, 'because that's the raison d'être of drama: Catharsis, purification. Isn't that its God-given task of old?'[12] However, not everyone felt that way as soon became clear when the play was on for more than two months. Otto got cold feet after 'several people had appealed to him' to cancel or postpone a Dutch staging. Otto quickly tried to sugarcoat his bad tidings: 'My advice would be not to rush, have the play brought to other countries first and wait for the feedback.' When Otto met the Hacketts in Basel, he convinced them to follow this route on the condition that when the time had come, Rob's ensemble should be chosen. Rob's first inclination was to travel to Basel to plead his case, but he soon realized this would be futile. But then he resumed his efforts under pressure of the upcoming season. It was time he got hold of a script. Even more so when he overheard that Otto had been in the country without notifying him. It was January and moving toward February. When Mr. Frank didn't respond, he tried with the Hacketts' agent, sending her a review in which Mr. Kugler talked ardently about the New York play. The message of course was not to worry about some nit-picker. If Mr. Kugler was satisfied, why bother? Finally, in the last week of February, Mr. Frank and De Vries met in Amsterdam for the first time.[13] It was the beginning of a warm relationship.

Survivors' shame and anger

In the interlude between the American and the European productions, fellow survivors gave Rob and Otto an earful. And some went public. The devastating op-ed came from (Matthew) Ies Spetter. Together with Etty Hillesum, Spetter smuggled children out of Westerbork, and together with Loe de Jong's twin brother Sally, he had tried to flee to Free Europe and then ended up in Drancy and Auschwitz. While Otto awaited the Russian army, Spetter joined a death march to Gleiwitz where he was liberated – Sally was killed. Spetter testified at the Nuremberg trials and migrated to the United States where he graduated and worked as a psychologist. Here someone spoke out with tremendous moral authority. His article appeared in *Vrij Nederland*, the magazine that, like *Het Parool*, was founded in the Resistance.[14] A typical product of the entertainment industry, the play was a 'sacrilege' and driven by effect. Spetter had been annoyed by the character drawings of Otto, the amiable and wise Jew, and voluptuous Anne. It was neither right to stage the Holocaust nor right to use affection to serve up the drama, by appealing to clichés or any other dramaturgical device even to the extent that spectators wiped the tears from their eyes with laughter. Anne Frank was not to be watched, said Spetter in words that were reminiscent of the cautious protest against the first Westerbork monument. 'Anne should not be put on display.' Spetter's criticism made it clear that the pain of the Shoah was now suddenly and too literally put in the spotlight. At least Rob had guessed that right.

The outcome of the dramatization was the product of the American culture industry and some even maintained that improper commercialization had already begun with the diary publication or in any case with Mr. Frank's promotional activities. Willy Pos – playwright and director of the Amsterdam drama school – was another survivor critic. With a hint of paternalism, Pos first acknowledged Rob's 'ideal' admitting 'that our dilapidated, afflicted and commercialized theater must rely on manifestations like this one to ever regain its original splendor.' Yet he did so only to reject Rob's efforts all the more harshly. Pos abhorred the vulgar display of recent suffering as if, paradoxically, De Vries thought he could liberate theater from commodification through a commercial injection. His objections were also personal. At the Jewish Secondary, Pos had taught Anne, 'the small, slender girl,' to 'parsing sentences, spelling, and the fundamentals of the belles-lettres.'[15]

Spetter was concerned not only with the ethics of representation as such but also with the chosen symbolism. In the appreciation of the interaction between the annexants and the helpers, a crucial disagreement, if not an unbridgeable chasm, between some survivors and the non-Jewish population became visible. This was related to the topos of 'poor Jews at the mercy of helpful "Aryans".' Just think of the opening scene in which a pregnant Miep shows compassion and behaves utterly protective toward Otto. The image of a childlike Anne could be extended to all annexants and thus encourage a maternal subject position from the audience. Dutch critics smugly remarked how German spectators would finally appreciate the courage of the Dutch to help their fellow Jewish citizens. Apart from the fact that Miep Gies was of Austrian descent, these critics seemed to have forgotten that the annexants were rounded up and sent to Auschwitz. In the public sphere, the Dutch still took the same high moral ground as just after the war when gratitude was the desired Jewish response; for example, when a 'Monument to Jewish Gratitude' (concerning the aid of non-Jewish citizens) was erected near the Jewish Secondary. Today it is more obvious how this type of mnemonic acts could be perceived as screens to obscure unwanted memories of complicity. The same could be said of the play. Spetter must have found the play complacent, for although it thematized the persecution, the audience basically was left off the hook and reassuringly told that deep down it was good at heart. Rob appreciated the script's potential to break through a defensive resistance and unlock unwanted memories, Spetter felt offensively interpellated by the cliché of Jewish passivity and gratitude – a recurrent specter of anti-Jewish stereotyping.

'The flip side of pity is contempt' and pity offered thus little attraction to many survivors.[16] Promoting the figuration of a bunch of Jews in hiding rescued by a team of benevolent helpers then amounted to an insulting cliché, the alleged lack of Jewish resistance; a stereotype for which Spetter and De Vries were living proof to the contrary. These objections got to be framed in terms of a Jewishness that was especially propagated in Israel and projected on an assumed submissive 'Ghetto mentality' that would have captivated the Jews for centuries. The Eichmann trial is the best-known catalyst for this topic but already before there were some painful issues – of which the assumption that Otto Frank should have worked his way out of the arrest became notorious.[17] It can even be traced back to Bialik's poetry of rage. Harry Mulisch alluded to these discussions when in his report on the Eichmann trial he mentioned the alleged indifference for Anne's diary in Israel. The author repeated the claim when the play was aired on national television: 'The book is hardly for sale in the country' because they 'abhor Jews who pose as pitiable. Jews need to thump.'[18]

The complaint of passivity was recapped in other writings, yet without taking into account that Anne's determination was in itself far from passive. In fact, as has been said, 'she wrote her housemates back into history.'[19] Still, the cloak of victimhood is not easy to wear. It can be shameful and demeaning, as Abram de Swaan (whose parents hid two blocks from Anne) explained in a lecture to commemorate the 50th anniversary of the Anne Frank House: 'In the *moral universe* all shame is on the oppressors and the executioners, the victims are due credit. But in the *emotional world* . . . it is the defeated who are ashamed.' The sociologist added that Anne Frank, being 'exceptionally emotionally gifted,' actually intimated these sentiments of shame in her diary.[20]

To the best of my knowledge, it has never been noticed that 'shame' is the very last word in the play, as spoken by Otto Frank: 'She puts me to shame.' Apparently, the Hacketts wished to send spectators of all sides and persuasions home with a moral and affective imperative uttered by the ghost of Anne. Each spectator could fill this in at his own discretion – the perpetrator who admits guilt, the bystander who feels implicated for not intervening – yet for survivors the closing sentence drew a line in the sand. It was as if for them the performance did not epitomize their (lack of) action but an objectified self. As a follow-up to Anne's buoyancy – speaking her aphorism to us from an unseen presence, Otto's shame left little room for 'inappropriate' survivor emotions such as feelings of misery, anger or resentment. The play put the survivor in the spotlight, yet it did so by aligning it with specific preferred, if not prescribed, emotions. Its forward-looking utopian message foregrounded forgiveness and demanded the overcoming of 'bad feelings' that supposedly kept humanity in the past.[21]

A Dutch adaptation

After the first German bookings, the Dutch ensemble received the green light. Opening night was set for November 27. Rob was looking forward to it, as he updated Otto. 'The play incites the passions. We were aware of that for a long time. It arouses huge interest and we do everything in our might to turn it into a major event. The preparations are in full swing.'[22] Rob was certainly out to create a buzz and some outside resistance couldn't hurt.

In August, the mail delivered two envelopes from New York: inside were the 'final script' including the stage instructions, a list of props, a blueprint of the set and photos of the costumes. Now it really started. Here's what the ensemble had to do 'to turn it into a major event': translate the script, build a set, collect props, prepare a soundscape ('Make our own montage! In triplicate – Frankf. & Vienna!' as Guttmann noted with foresight), record Anne's voice 'as if coming from the air' and assemble a cast. And, not to be forgotten, start rehearsing. Rob was already busy with the challenge of an Amsterdam premiere. Otto was deeply involved and wished to be kept informed.

When Rob de Vries received a not-yet-definitive copy of the script a few months earlier, one of the country's most respected critics 'coincidentally' got his hands on it. Apparently, the steam came out of his ears because the Jewish critic Hans Gomperts immediately wrote a devastating op-ed in *Het Parool*, the newspaper that was so intimately linked to the diary and the war. The play was trite, Anne too glamorously portrayed and fictions had been added – 'even the diary quotes were fabrications.' In an original observation, the critic had determined that the script was written to the taste of Central European American Jews in its portrayal of two cowardly Dutchmen rather than focusing on the generational struggles of two German exile families that Anne had so masterfully recorded. Let's hope the country will be spared from this sentimental kitsch.

This was at a time when De Vries had some issues to keep his ensemble going and Guttmann put on a play that he considered to be the pièce de resistance of his career. It must have been difficult, then, to bear the harsh criticism that came in, even before the play went public. Karl's notes show Gomperts's review had landed. Now it was to be decided how to respond.

The critic was concerned not only with the script but with adaptations in general, 'the poverty of our time.' Pretty much everything that mattered in modern literature – inner thoughts and feelings – would disappear in the wave of stage adaptations that swept the theater world. It was a classic take on a stage adaptation as a surrogate, a poor replacement for the original. Yet, as critic Gomperts thought out loud, 'maybe it's all about the performance.' Maybe adaptations met with the longing for 'nostalgia for a homogeneous, collective culture' at a time of rapid modernization. People want so much to be together, share and undergo their experiences collectively to work on their 'healing' that they prefer theater as a supplement to the intimacy of reading. First you read about Kafka's distressed souls, then you undergo and re-experience his confessions of solitude in unison. And that's where De Vries and Guttmann's efforts would begin, that is, in the production of a play in which actors and spectators indeed meet and share their experiences and thus collectively work through their pain. Or, as Karl explained: that's what drama is all about. 'I believe in the cathartic effect of experiencing together' and 'this play was a textbook example.' Faced with the multifaceted criticism, Rob called on Karl to take his time and put on a play 'that would do the Jews good' and prove critic Gomperts wrong – or right when it came to the added value of theater.[23]

Adjustments to satisfy the critics began with the script. The ensemble's dramaturg Anty Westerling translated the script while Karl gathered background information, comparing the script to historical events. The moment the final script had arrived, he called Otto Frank to ask him some questions, like *Tagebuch wie sah es aus*? Diary what did it look like? Karl was interested in biographical details, the ages of the adults and the like. He discussed Margot's character with Otto because her role and personality were so underexposed – a present absence. He was very much interested in the chronology. For instance, on how events did follow after Otto's return. Karl made a list with biographical data, occasionally with the name of an eligible actor written along. From the script he took it that Otto was a gentle European and Edith was gentle bred, which according to Karl meant that she came '*aus guter Familie*.' Dussel was finicky, which Guttmann translated as '*pedantisch*' (in German) and '*piete-peuterig*' (in Dutch). *Piete-peuterig*, meticulously punctilious in his preparations, that was also said of Guttmann as a director. If Rob was known for his social engagement, Karl stood for professional competent dramatizations – doing justice to the script such as stressing a faithful delivery of the lines. Karl linked all passages in the script to the chronology of the diary and tried to date everything as accurately as possible, which he then graphed.

Combining the new information into a translation was the next step in adapting, or rather appropriating, the adaptation. It has been incorrectly noted that the ensemble would follow the American script slavishly.[24] The Dutch script would contain various minor amendments, but it was indeed not the case that Westerling came to the type of changes in the dialogues for which the French translator was severely reprimanded by the Hacketts.[25] It stuck to various minor and major incorrections or notable omissions. Nor did Westerling change the highly contested permutation of the April 11, 1944, quotation on Jews as a persecuted people: 'We're not the only people that've had to suffer . . . sometimes one race . . . sometimes another.' Westerling's translation was mainly a re-translation to a Dutch original with a few key changes and various minor ones. For words that were Anglicized, the original words had to be retrieved. These would be the terms that would resonate with the spectators, words that they may not have heard for a long time and would deliver an emotional pinprick: *distributiekaarten, bonkaarten, Grünen, moffen.*

The first notable amendment is the nationality of Dussel. In the original script, Dussel was Dutch: 'This has been such a shock to me. I'd always thought of myself as Dutch. I was born in Holland. My father was born in Holland, and my grandfather. And now . . . after all these years.' In the Dutch script, this has been shortened to as follows: 'I'm still a bit confused. . . . I've lived here for so many years.' Critic Gomperts got his way. When handing out presents in the crucial Hanukkah scene, Dussel does not say: 'Like *our* St Nicolas Day,' but, 'Just like with Sinterklaas.' Criticism was clearly taken to heart, even though Dussel's American lines would have made for an interesting intervention into the postwar debate on the alleged integration of Dutch Jewry. In the German staging, Guttmann stuck to '*Wie bei uns zu Nikolaus*.' After consulting with Mr. Frank, Guttmann had included it in his biographical notes: *alle Personen, ausser Miep und Kraler, sind deutsche Emigranten* but he deleted all traces of the forced migration, emphatically omitting a stage instruction concerning the German accents (as he also deleted the German *knix* or curtsy as a form of greeting for young girls that like Anne's German dress had already been recognized as 'fairly undutch').[26] In fact, Miep originally came from Austria and Kugler from the German-speaking part of the Czech Republic. Only Voskuijl and Kleiman were native Dutch.

According to the script, Dussel was not only Dutch, but also secular and quite annoying. Karl and Otto spoke on the phone about Dussel whom they called by his real name Fritz Pfeffer. Otto explained that in the beginning Pfeffer was a very sympathetic man (Guttmann: '!!!'), but who in hiding became lonely and miserable and who developed some serious mood swings. Otto told him that Pfeffer's wife Charlotte Kaletta was actually living in the Netherlands and his son from a previous marriage had been sent to England on a Kindertransport. Dussel did not live alone. In the critical edition, readers would learn about Anne acknowledging Pfeffer's wife and disapprovingly telling about his secret correspondence with her while in hiding. This was taken up in the Wendy Kesselman script revision when Dussel regained his rightful married status.[27]

Karl and Rob were already informed of Pfeffer's circumstances in 1956. Arguably, the information provided by Otto may have urged actor Bernard Droog to mimic Dussel 'very sincerely' as his colleague Anne-Marie Heyligers put it, as much tortured as his co-annexants and not nearly as caricatured as the part might have been. But Dussel remained single. The figure of 'Dussel' would continue to haunt the play and the feature film. The depiction of the dentist came to a head in the Hanukkah celebration where he was portrayed as being ignorant about Jewish rituals – which he definitely was not. In the Kesselman script, he regained his piety including a tallit for his daily prayers in Hebrew. Pfeffer had an Orthodox upbringing and did become liberal only later in life. Just after opening night, Rob did receive a letter from a friend of the Pfeffers. As Mrs. Pfeffer had tried in vain to explain to Otto, she was utterly disappointed with the play, with the Hanukkah scene and with the way Otto and the ensemble had handled her complaints.[28] Mrs. Pfeffer grew bitter for being ignored. After her death, an employee of the Anne Frank House found her belongings (photo's, letters), including the program notes of the Dutch play, at a street market.[29]

The Dutch dramatization contains a second major intervention. In the final script, the song and the prayers were in English. Karl introduced Hebrew as a ritual language. The song *Oh Hanukkah Oh Hanukkah* was to be translated into the prevailing language of each country. 'Oh Hanukkah sweet celebration' thus became the German '*Oh Chanukka, ihr herrlichen Tage*.' Anne mentions 'the song' in her diary but without providing a title. Otto identified the song as *Ma'oz Tzur*, yet Kanin got his way with the more upbeat song *Oh Hanukkah*. A Hebrew song would alienate Broadway audiences, and either way a jubilant song would work better in contrast to the upcoming drama.[30] The play would go from the complex excitement of jubilant singing, bonding and fear in the Hanukkah scene to the depressed and stressed atmosphere in the first scene after the break. Karl went along with this as can be inferred from a marginale for the latter scene in his prompt book: 'All! Hunger! Fear! Dejection! *Alle gehen einander auf die Nerven!* (Everyone gets on each other's nerves!).'

When the annexants celebrated their first Hanukkah in hiding, the newspaper of the Dutch Jewish Council was also discussing the Hanukkah songs: 'Every Jew in Central and Western Europe' knows *Ma'oz Tzur*, 'the most popular of all Jewish melodies.'[31] Except for those in the secret annex if the US team had its way. In September 1956, Karl received an ukase from Otto and Fischer Verlag that included the mandatory German lines of *Oh Hanukkah* for all German productions, but he nevertheless adopted *Ma'oz Tzur* in the Dutch staging. Judging by the German prompt books, he did comply with 'the only authorized version' in his German-language productions.

In modern criticism of the script, the song choice is presented as evidence of the producers bowing to a non-Jewish or secular Broadway audience. But that might be a little bit too simplistic. *Ma'oz Tzur* does indeed fit the Dutch Jewish community, but it also signals a Western European Ashkenazi Judaism. *Oh Hanukkah* may have been in English, but it went back to the Yiddish *Oy Khanukkah* and thus also stood for Eastern European Jewishness, which perhaps made it more truthful or authentic than it seems at first glance.[32] In fact, both songs had gone through a complex nineteenth- and twentieth-century European and American history of appropriation that included various melodies.[33] Still, *Ma'oz Tzur* fitted the German-Dutch Jews in the secret annex and was recognizable for most Jewish spectators.

There were some tough nuts to crack with regard to the prayers too. There's an opening and a closing prayer from Otto (that is, due to an intervention by Guttman, the last prayer was transferred from Van Daan to Mr. Frank). These were three customary prayers. Again a small amendment was implemented. The prayers would be recited first in Hebrew then in Dutch. As part of the reenactment, the Hacketts have Mrs. Frank recite a psalm for which they chose Psalm 121, 'I lift mine eyes unto the mountains.' Halfway the burglary, Edith was to repeat the first lines. This time Karl conformed to a Dutch recitation but to validate this, he inserted a line in which Otto explicitly requested Edith to recite the psalm in translation.[34] Karl deleted a second recitation and instead have Edith recite the *Shema Yisrael* prayer – in Hebrew – which Edith should call out *Intensiv, mit Kraft*. A transcription of this vital Jewish prayer was added to the prompt book.

'Dear Mr. De Vries, 'Could you please inform me which Jewish festival was celebrated and which part of the Bible was read so beautifully?'[35] Not everyone in the cast will have been familiar with the ritual either. Karl and Rob certainly did, Mols and Crefcoeur will have been aware with the ceremony as such. Jules Croiset was still able to mumble the first lines of the song 60 years later, but he knew next to nothing about it at the time of the play. Heyligers had experienced a few ritual moments through a Jewish friend, but she didn't know the song. During rehearsals, cheat sheets with the text transcribed phonetically were available for all actors.

In his dramatization, Karl was able to amplify some of the traces in the script. His interventions helped to convey the sentiment that there were Jews onstage and thus answered the oft-asked question of how spectators knew the characters were Jewish at all – after having removed their yellow badges. Much more than the American version, the ensemble tried to evoke the force of Jewishness under the pressure of oppression. With the prayers came the significant lines about the heroic Maccabees, 2,000 years ago, who fought 'against indifference, against tyranny and oppression,' closed off by Psalm 121. The scene was concluded with *Ma'oz Tzur*. Next: Intermission.

Typecasting

The reenactment of Hanukkah became paradoxically more truthful by portraying Pfeffer as less knowledgeable in order to give relief to the Jewishness of the others. Enhancing the reality effect – that is aroused by adding seemingly insignificant details – also played out in the casting that should follow the casting strategy of typecasting. Casting, in a sense, got connected with other strategies of concealing the theatricality of the play. On the other hand, by emphasizing typecasting, the show actually subtextually commented on the contemporary conventions for drama.

The casting had started months earlier. In his early letters, Rob already pointed out the urgency of contracting actors to speed up Otto's decision-making. In the Netherlands, the ensemble was the organizational unity of drama, which meant that the choice of scripts depended on the availability of actors by age, gender, type and acting style. The members of the ensemble earned a fixed salary as employees. Rob wished to circumvent these institutional restrictions aiming for a cast that came as close as possible to the historical figures. Typecasting was key, but as a casting practice it was rather novel in the Netherlands. Karl and Rob would look for the appropriate actors in and outside of the ensemble.

Typecasting was not yet seen as a practice of pigeonholing actors in certain stage types, but as an instrument to achieve a certain degree of realism.[36] In 1955, it was discussed as the latest fashion from England and the United States.[37] Typecasting would transport the spectators back in time who would give up their defenses when confronted with a theatrical three-dimensional multimedia spectacle that seduces them to believe in the genuineness of Anne and Otto onstage. The performance gains authority not only by historicizing actors and set but also by watching actors with the appropriate background. Public knowledge of the actors' tragic or heroic biographies could be a way to get wrapped up by the performance. Ghosting, calling out the spirits from the past hidden behind the perceptible actors onstage, was a double-edged sword. And so was typecasting. About Rob in his role as Otto, it was said he would actually reenact his own life on stage.

Rob and Karl had months to cast but seven weeks before opening night, the cast was still incomplete. Karl kept a list of names, Rob wrote letters to persuade candidates or, if necessary, jumped in his car to visit candidates at home. It all began with Anne. Things went more modest in the Netherlands than abroad with some large-scale auditions, yet none the less intensive. Once found, the belief quickly arose that a better actress would never be found. In the 1980s, Jeroen Krabbé regularly spoke with Guttmann about a new production, but the director did not see how a suitable actress could ever be found. He was still thinking about his Anne.[38]

Already at the first attempt to obtain the rights, Rob de Vries thought of a specific actress who 'in appearance and mindset and talent, will be the only one able to play the part in our country,' as he explained to Otto. Ellen van Hemert was through family ties connected with theater and television. Her father would produce the 1962 TV recording. At one point, 20-year-old Martine Crefcoeur entered the picture. She was still in drama school and the management didn't want to let her go as it was against procedure and habit to place a pupil in a carrying role. She was on the radar early on when Rob attended a series of freshman exams in which the upcoming actress assisted and probably from that moment on had his eyes on her talent.[39]

The Dutch theater system did not provide for the casting of a suitable 13–17-year-old actress. Eligible candidates could only be found from within the network of professionals. In light of the ideal of typecasting, it was also suggested that casting should aim not only at young but also at inexperienced candidates. Rob had thus requested photographer Maria Austria to audition her orphaned niece. All the same, on August 29 Van Hemert was engaged, 14 days after the final script had arrived. Rob welcomed her with a birthday present: a 'chronicle' of the persecution of the Dutch Jews by the Jewish publicist and inmate of Bergen-Belsen, Abel Herzberg. Van Hemert was 'pleasantly surprised' and hoped that it would help her to gain some insight into 'the atmosphere and the time, which are of course quite vague to me, so it will enable me to fulfil my artistic mission properly.' The actress got invited to a private audience with Otto Frank.[40]

Surprisingly, after the contract was signed, the selection started all over again. Karl organized an audition in The Hague with four candidates. By now the preparations were in the first week of October.[41] Both Van Hemert and Crefcoeur, as an understudy, showed up at the first reading, a few days after October 10 and both joined the ensuing intensive period of rehearsals. Then came the public announcement that Van Hemert was pregnant and withdrew from the production. Under pressure of the circumstances, the drama school changed tack and released Crefcoeur. Now it was her turn to be presented to the press. Crefcoeur would do the entire tour while continuing her drama lessons. For the first few months, she played Anne while she rehearsed for *Romeo and Juliet* during the day and traveled up and down the train all week, only to occasionally settle in a hotel.

De Vries was happy with the outcome because Crefcoeur 'came closest' to his image of Anne.[42] Jules Croiset gave a retrospective explanation. Van Hemert was a 'good actress and a lovely woman,' but 'very blond' and not well suited to the rest of the family. Crefcoeur was a better fit, and, as incidentally noted in the Jewish Weekly, also ‘half-Jewish.’ The latter was rarely mentioned in the newspapers, but it may well have been part of Karl and Rob’s considerations. In a letter to the editor in the same journal, it was lamented that the Jewish background of the actress was not taken into account: why not try a little harder and find someone ‘who’s been through it all.’ Crefcoeur was described as having ‘a slight resemblance’ to Anne, but also as not looking very Jewish.[43] The actress did not feel the need to fill in on her background. She did voice some concerns about her Rotterdam accent though – and took speech lessons.[44]

It was common for ensembles to assail drama schools in search of young talent, and this is also how Crefcoeur’s theater sister was found: Anne-Marie Heyligers had graduated from drama school a few months earlier and her exam play actually functioned as an audition.[45] She was determined to obtain an assignment with De Haagse Comedie of which she had attended all performances from the cheap upper gallery. However, her husband, who was already employed there (and that was how she also knew Guttmann), was told that ‘tying’ was not in the habit of the ensemble. And so they went to Arnhem ‘in exile.’

The third youth was Jules Croiset, 19 years old, son and grandson of famous actors. He had already made his debut, but Peter was to be his first major role. Croiset had to audition, this time with a member of the board but that was just a formality. A year before he had been at a ‘dreadful audition’ with Guttmann. Croiset never went to drama school and had to make do with a few acting lessons from his father. Father Max had suggested auditioning at De Haagse Comedie for when he finished high school. *Enter*: Karl Guttmann. Jules’s selection of ‘heavy texts’ couldn’t fascinate Guttmann or anything else for that matter as he was actually clearing his desk for almost the entire audition only interrupting his pursuits by asking *Haben sie noch etwas* or concluding *Sie haben viel Talent, aber Sie müssen noch viel lernen.* A year later Croiset returned in the guise of Peter van Daan. Thanks to the success of the Anne Frank play, the ‘talented young man’ returned to De Haagse Comedie after all (as would Heyligers a few years later), causing the need for a replacement in the second season.[46]

Most of the adult parts were quickly filled in. Casting decisions were influenced by long-term bonds, war past and stage appearance. Otto was to be played by Rob. Enny Mols was hired from the radio broadcaster for the part of Mrs. Van Daan. The two were close. Both were Jewish with Mols pointing out that she became aware of her Jewish roots ‘only after Hitler came to power.’[47] The three gentlemen knew each other well and they were of impeccable standing in terms of their war past as even *The New York Times*’ reviewer cared to mention. Bernhard (‘Bob’) Droog’s biography mirrored that of Herman van Pels: Dutch yet born and raised in Nazi

Figure 7 The director and the cast – except for the two helpers – during rehearsals, November 1956. The placement follows the Hanukkah scene (Maria Austria/MAI)

Germany. He fled to the Netherlands in the 1930s, served in the resistance and performed forced labor in a German camp. Hans Tiemeijer (Mr. Van Daan) was a former Spanish Civil War and resistance fighter. He had been imprisoned in Scheveningen – at the same time as De Vries, and in Vught and Dachau. Like Enny Mols, De Vries knew Tiemeijer from a few plays in the early years of the war.

This left one part. In an early stage, the well-known actress Mieke Verstraete who happened to be Croiset's aunt, was sounded out for the role of Mrs. Frank. After two months, she returned the contract unsigned 'due to specific unforeseen circumstances.' On Guttmann's list was scribbled behind her name: *goed in de oorlog??* ('good during the war??'), but it remains unclear how this relates to her withdrawal.[48] When the Jewish actress Heleen Pimentel declined, Jenny van Maerlant, a permanent ensemble member, was offered the part.[49]

Affective memories at the rehearsals

Sometime around October 14, the cast got together for a read-through of the script. Until then, stage actors had not had access to the script. Seated around a table in the rehearsal room, the script was read from front to back. In a way it's a first performance. For a moment, the cast became an audience put in a position to let its thoughts go over the play.

It was up to Karl Guttmann to deliver the reading. After reciting Bialik in Vienna, Yiddish poetry in Russia and Werfel's German script in Palestine – all under strained circumstances, he found himself in a rehearsal room in Arnhem with the playscript of the Hacketts in front of him. The director was already in preparation for months, but this was the first time all cast members met. The older actors had been involved in the Dutch smalltown theater world for a long time. Martine Crefcoeur was new to the scene. Anne-Marie Heyligers was performing in her first play at the time of the rehearsals and thus already saw a few familiar faces when stepping into the rehearsal room. She did not know the two actresses for the part of Anne and they exchanged a few words. Then Guttmann took the floor.

The moment the director commenced his reading, it began to dawn: the ensemble was about to perform a play about genuine people who had only recently died. Was that even appropriate? Heyligers had read the diary a few years before and was surprised by the quality of the writing: it was moving and witty at the same time. But she couldn't quite figure out how to turn that into a play and she had to wait months before finally getting the chance to gain an answer:

> I suddenly realized that we were going to be impersonating people who had died and not only that, they had been murdered in the most horrible way. That flashed through my head and stifled me in these very first moments of the reading.

This is Mrs. Heyligers who, at the age of 89, looks back on the play at home in her postwar modernist apartment building in The Hague in which she came to live when she finally joined De Haagse Comedie. It can be read as a very personal belief, but also shows the novelty of the event: the Shoah on stage. When the disturbing feeling sunk in, she did not know what to do and got distracted:

> Rob de Vries and Karl Guttmann and Anty Westerling were so convinced that this play had to be performed because, well, yes, in addition to that diary, people had to know what happened or they wanted to wake them up again. . . . They did not seem to think about whether that was allowed. It had to, it was an assignment, a sacred assignment, certainly from Rob's point of view. And that was such a barrier to speak out.

There was a generation gap running through the cast, the three young actors at one side and the 'adults' at the other. Heyligers saw that the young ones – 'well, I was already twenty-five' – had their own thoughts. Croiset came to the same conclusion independent of Heyligers. He saw himself together with Crefcoeur as the real youth. Heyligers seemed older to him – which was correct – and more grown-up. Croiset remembers the rehearsals that were etched into his memory as 'a quite eventful period' or rather as 'one big knot of emotion.' The rehearsals were intensive and complicated for Croiset for more than one reason. Ensemble members were expected to settle down in Arnhem. Heyligers was immediately offered a three-room apartment. Yet Croiset continued living in Amsterdam because he took Arnhem for 'a terrible place,' Heyligers called it intolerably middle class in its standards. Croiset 'hitchhiked up and down because you earned next to nothing.' Only now and then could he afford a train ticket. Croiset stepped into the rehearsal room eagerly. Heyligers's moral objections – later supplemented with artistic ones – were foreign to him. He had just finished his first roles in a youth ensemble and Peter was his big part and breakthrough. In the rehearsal room, he was confronted with actors who could not control their emotions. 'The war was still fresh in their minds, the horrors of the Nazis, the gasses, but Martine and I, we were like children, we reacted to these vehement responses.' That already started with the read-through, as Heyligers remembers. 'The elderly were blubbing. Jenny van Maerlant, I remember very well, Rob with tears in his eyes. I couldn't cry, I didn't have any tears.'

The actors expressed themselves emotionally with crying fits during rehearsals. They also began to tell their own stories in a very emotional way. Croiset: 'We instead wanted to enjoy acting. Despite the fact that I had experienced it myself with my father, in a hiding of sorts in Friesland, away from my hometown. But we were young.' Maybe the war was still too close. In any case, it led to many conflicts. Or perhaps not exactly: it was rather that 'the youth' got a bit 'rowdy' toward all that adult seriousness.

The rehearsals were also affected by current events during the Cold War, which is a fine example of the sliding of signs from one event to the other. The outside world in the guise of the Hungarian Uprising seeped through during rehearsals and that required another whistle call. Guttmann publicly stated three days before the premiere that the actors had been inspired by the crushing of the rebellion: 'There was an unusual spirit at rehearsals, and an aspiration to propagate Anne Frank's ideal.'[50] Empathy with the oppressed Hungarians of which many fled to the Netherlands went far. The Communists had become the Nazis. The Amstel Avenue in the Rivierenbuurt – located next to Merwede Square – was one of three avenues that were given the names of the allied leaders during the war. In 1956, after the Soviet intervention in the Hungarian Uprising, Stalin Avenue was renamed again, this time it became Freedom Avenue. Early November, people secretly swapped

Stalin Av. for 'November 4 Av.' – the date of the Russian intervention – even before the city council had decided on the name change. The analogy between the persecution and the Russian intervention would surface in reviews and comments: 'An equally cruel terror weighs on human happiness a few hundred miles from here.'[51]

Rob was quite satisfied with the rehearsals and he kept Otto posted: the rehearsals 'take place with the greatest dedication and concentration that I have experienced so far.' But sometimes they appeared more to be like therapeutic sessions. Hans Tiemeijer saw the storyline got mixed up with his own memories of a raid in Amsterdam when a rabbi and his family, including his daughter's girlfriend, were taken before his eyes.[52]

The emotional outburst among some of the older members of the cast deviate from the emotional mood of silence and restraint that would characterize these years. It appears that the play and the act of performing could break the silence. According to a 'hydraulic vision,' emotions usually are taken for 'great liquids within each person heaving and frothing, eager to be let out.' In common language, emotions flow are channeled or erupt. But, as historian Barbara Rosenwein argued, affective dispositions can be better understood as shaped, managed and expressed in social interaction.[53] Taking this idea to the rehearsal room, we could surmise that the emotions were not simply there waiting to be let out. They were created in the togetherness of the rehearsals. One step further and the events during rehearsals might even be construed as part of the collective process of bringing a play into production instead of the outcome of unfortunate and unwanted outbursts. The actors would then have been invited to draw on their affective memory, as known by the approach of dramatist Konstantin Stanislavski and his students. By means of an emotional recall, actors go back to feelings attached to events from their own life and apply these in their role. So when much later, after more than 200 performances, a German ensemble intends to visit the Netherlands, Rob argues against the show. 'All the actors may have been cleared, but still I don't want to think about who is banging on the door at the end of the play.' Talk about typecasting! While acknowledging that he spoke out in 'fairly emotional' terms, Rob defended his position by admitting that these were the same indispensable sentiments that had contributed to the ensemble's success.[54] Some cast members explicitly told their experiences during rehearsals and at one time a photo of Tiemeijer who was locked up in Dachau circulated. 'Extremely thin, lying in a kind of crate. I was very overwhelmed by that picture, especially because he was such a sturdy man,' as Croiset remembers vividly.

Memories and emotions were introduced that were linked to the war, even if it was not to every one's taste.[55] To be sure. The young ones did have their own war experiences. Croiset had to cope with a complex family history. His parents were divorced in the beginning of the occupation. His father went into hiding in his hometown, The Hague. Jules and his brother Hans (who was on Guttmann's list for the play and who would star in Max Frisch's 1961 play *Andorra*) were sent into the province separated from both parents. Jules was 9 when the war ended, and, as already mentioned, his father struggled with the loss of family and friends. Martine Crefcoeur was 10 when the war ended. Her mother's family was badly affected by the Shoah. In an interview, she recalled how her mother's Jewish parents were taken: 'It's strange that a critic wrote that Anne's Jewishness was missing from how I played her. I didn't deliberately look for it either.'

Anne-Marie Heyligers grew up in the Dutch East Indies where she was imprisoned in two camps set up by the Japanese occupiers. After the war, she came to the Netherlands. She recalls the war was never discussed at school, not even by children who were known to have been imprisoned. 'It could not get through to you. Or maybe you wanted to ignore it because it might lead to your own experiences.' She reminisces: 'Once I was in a waiting room and flipped through a magazine, and suddenly I saw a photo of stacks of corpses. I was so shocked and then I thought this can't be true.' Nor did Anne's diary seem related to the photos. This of course was exactly what critics would stress: the noble feelings expressed in the diary and especially the play left no room for the horror of the camps.

At a school reunion in 2002, Heyligers suggested to her former classmates to write short autobiographies. Only then did she discover that some classmates had been in camps just like her. At the time of rehearsals, she did not talk about the war and was extremely annoyed by Tiemeijer's constant 'tall stories' of which she believed at most half.

All in all, the reading took a different course. The usual discussion and planning were quickly abandoned. Whereas Heyligers wondered where she had ended up, Rob radiated the devotion and piety he had promised Otto Frank. 'After Guttmann concluded his reading of the play,' as he pronounced,

> we were all deeply impressed, were silent for minutes and then left quietly, with tears in our eyes, but not just with feelings of vengeance or with feelings of hatred because these sentiments are not intimated by the play at all. What is generated much more strongly is love, the play is about love, the love for your fellow human beings.[56]

Rob's take on Karl's reading was a preview of the atmosphere during the premiere.

Notes

1 GA 0644, 183: Frank to De Vries, October 16, 1955; radio report, November 26, 1956 via *Andere Tijden*, NPO TV, February 20, 2016, www.anderetijden.nl; GA 0644, 183: De Vries to Querido-Pimentel, September 25, 1956.
2 Hanny Alkema, 'Heleen Pimentel 1916–2008,' *Trouw*, August 13, 2008.
3 Interview Ensel – Croiset, Amsterdam, June 25, 2020; Max Croiset, *6 000 000* (Amsterdam, 1965).
4 *De Telegraaf*, December 23, 1953 or even before: *Algemeen Dagblad*, August 1, 1952; GA 0644, 183: De Vries to Frank, January 22, 1957.
5 Dirk Gindt, 'Transatlantic translations and transactions: Lars Schmidt and the implementation of postwar American theatre in Europe,' *Theatre Journal* 65, 1 (2013): 19–37.
6 'The boonies' in: GA 0644, 9: overview of Theater in the first three years of its existence (October 25, 1956); *Arnhemsche Courant*, October 27, 1953.
7 De Vries did employ the word 'survivor' in a letter to the Hacketts' agent Leah Salisbury (GA 0644, 183: February 12, 1956). On the survivor, see: Kristin Wagrell, *"Chorus of the saved": Constructing the Holocaust survivor in Swedish public discourse, 1943–1966* (Linköping, 2020) (on Anne Frank, 193–254).
8 Veto in *De Telegraaf*, February 18, 1956; *The New York Times*, November 30, 1956.
9 KG: New York program notes; for the Burgtheater visit, see: *Het Volk*, May 21, 1942; *De Telegraaf*, September 14, 1955.
10 *De Telegraaf*, February 18, 1956; GA 0644, 183: De Vries to Frank, October 12, 1955; David Barnouw, *The phenomenon of Anne Frank* (Bloomington, 2018), 37.
11 GA 0644, 183: De Vries to Frank, December 5, 1955.
12 Review in KG: H. Koningburg, 'Zuivering op de planken van het New-Yorkse toneel' (additional references are missing), New York program notes.
13 GA 0644, 183: Frank to De Vries, December 9 and 14, 1955; De Vries to Frank, December 29, 1955 and January 29, 1956; De Vries to Leah Salisbury, January 20, 23 and February 12, 1956 including a clipping of De Vries to Frank, February 11, 1956; Frank to De Vries, February 14, 1956.
14 Ies Spetter, 'Onderduikpret op Broadway: Onverdragelijk succes van Anne Franks dagboek,' *Vrij Nederland*, November 5, 1955; Bettine Sierksema, 'New light on Etty Hillesum's actions in Camp Westerbork,' in *The lasting significance of Etty Hillesum's writings*, ed. Klaas A.D. Smelik (Amsterdam, 2019), 341–352.
15 UvA: Brpost0008, Pos to De Vries, November 30, 1956; W.Ph. Pos, 'Dramatische Kroniek,' *Kroniek voor Kunst en Kultuur* 18 (1959).
16 Susan Lanzoni, *Empathy: A history* (New Haven, 2016), 29.
17 Bruno Bettelheim, 'The ignored lesson of Anne Frank,' *Harper's Magazine* 1 (1960): 45–50.
18 Harry Mulisch, *De zaak 40/61: Een reportage* (Amsterdam, 1962), 45; *De Telegraaf*, May 4, 1962.
19 Deborah E. Kaplan, 'Anne Frank, Reviser,' *Pedagogy* 19, 1 (2018): 87–107, 101.
20 Translation and emphasis added, re. Abram de Swaan, lecture: 'In de buurt van Anne Frank. Rede bij de viering van het 50-jarig bestaan van het Anne Frankhuis' (April 28, 2010) and e-mail, August 16, 2020.
21 Sara Ahmed, 'Happy objects,' in *The affect theory reader*, eds. Melissa Gregg and Gregory J. Seigworth (Durham, 2009), 29–51.

22 GA 0644 183: De Vries to Frank, September 21, 1956.
23 *NIW*, February 24, 1984.
24 Marian de Vooght, 'In the shadow of the diary: Anne Frank's fame and the effects of translation,' in *Translating Holocaust lives*, eds. Jean Boase-Beier et al. (London, 2017), 97–122.
25 David L. Goodrich, *The real Nick and Nora: Frances Goodrich and Albert Hackett, writers of stage and screen classics* (Carbondale, IL, 2004), 236.
26 *Nieuwsblad van het Noorden*, November 15, 1956.
27 Frances Goodrich and Albert Hackett, *The Diary of Anne Frank*. Newly adapted by Wendy Kesselman (New York, 2016, first edition, 1997), 29–33.
28 UvA: Brjooh001, Hans Joosten aan De Vries, December 2, 1957.
29 Joke Kniesmeijer in *Het Parool*, November 9, 1987; Nanda van der Zee, *De kamergenoot van Anne Frank* (Amsterdam, 1990).
30 The song was changed a week before opening night: Judah M. Cohen, 'Sounds from the secret annex. Composing a young girl's thoughts,' in *Anne Frank unbound: Media, imagination, memory*, eds. Barbara Kirshenblatt-Gimblett and Jeffrey Shandler (Bloomington, 2012), 265–287, 266.
31 *Joodsche Weekblad*, December 4, 1942.
32 Henriette Boas in *Algemeen Handelsblad*, April 24, 1959.
33 Dianne Ashton, *Hanukkah in America: A history* (New York and London, 2013).
34 KG: Prompt book, Vienna for bilingual blessing and added line for Otto to Edith.
35 UvA: Brheut001, H. Heuterman to De Vries, February 1, 1957.
36 Pamela Robertson Wojcik, 'Typecasting,' *Criticism* 45, 2 (2003): 223–249.
37 David Koning, 'Schijnwerpers zijn geen leeslampen,' *De Nieuwsgier*, December 12, 1955.
38 *Elseviers Magazine*, February 16, 1984.
39 *De Telegraaf*, November 2, 1956.
40 GA 0644 183: M.J. Kip to NRU, August 29, 1956; Van Hemert to De Vries, September 1, 1956; Kip to Guttmann, September 19, 1956; script for Van Hemert: note in KG; Press presentation: *Algemeen Dagblad*, September 19, 1956.
41 The two other candidates were Irene Fischer and Cecilia Lichtveld.
42 GA 0644, 15: Ensemble (Mr. Kip) to Crefcoeur, December 22, 1956; De Vries to NRU, November 3, 1956; GA 0644, 183: De Vries to Frank, November 8, 1956 on his ideal Anne.
43 *NIW*, November 30, 1956; *Het Vrije Volk*, January 14, 1957.
44 GA 0644, 183: Account for speech lessons, May 3, 1957.
45 Interview Ensel – Heyligers, June 30, 2020.
46 *Haags Gemeentearchief*, 0315-01, *De Haagse Kunststichting*, 597 Minutes of the board, May 15, 1957.
47 Henk van Gelder, 'Leeuwe, Engelina de,' in *Digitaal Vrouwenlexicon van Nederland*, http://resources.huygens.knaw.nl/vrouwenlexicon/lemmata/data/Leeuwe (accessed January 23, 2021) and UvA: Brleeuw02, Mols to Hoenderink, December 15, 1945.
48 GA 0644, 183: De Vries to Verstraete-Brusse, July 14, 1956; refusal note: August 12, 1956.
49 John de Freese and Mia Goossen took on the roles of the two helpers.
50 *Algemeen Dagblad*, November 24, 1956 (that is three days before the premiere).
51 *De Maasbode*, November 27, 1956. See also *De Tijd* and *Het Parool*, November 28, 1956. On Anne Frank in Hungary, see: Kata Bohus, 'Anne and Eva,

two diaries, two Holocaust memories in communist Hungary,' *Remembrance & Solidarity Studies* 5 (2016): 97–113.

52 B&G: radio show *De stand van zaken*, December 2, 1983; Henk van Gelder, 'Hans Tiemeijer 1908–1997. Idealistisch acteur,' *de Volkskrant*, October 13, 1997.

53 Barbara H. Rosenwein, 'Worrying about emotions in history,' *The American Historical Review* 107, 3 (2002): 821–845.

54 GA 0644, 183: De Vries to Bureau Theaterrechten, May 16, 1958.

55 Interview Ensel – Croiset, Amsterdam, June 25, 2020.

56 Radio report, November 26, 1956 via *Andere Tijden*, NPO TV, February 20, 2016, www.anderetijden.nl.

Figure 8 The Dutch set as conceived by Boris Aronson and adapted by Wim Vasseur (Maria Austria/MAI)

4 Driven by affect

Opening night and beyond

Go visit the play if your nerves can withstand the emotions.

–Hans Gomperts, critic

Opening night

Would the audience go along with the play's message of love that was announced on national radio? Was the aphoristic imperative uttered by Anne's ghost audible only by Otto or would it be absorbed by the spectators as well? Rob de Vries had to wait until the evening of November 27 for the beginning of an answer to that question. The radio call shows how the performance was prepped though. There must in fact have been quite a bit of anticipation from readers of the diary and from those who had read from skeptical and passionate critics about the staging abroad. The publisher's ad for the 11th edition (51,000–60,000) of the diary that appeared right at the time of the premiere echoed Rob's coda: 'love is discovered in this book, life flourishes, this booklet helps us believe in humanity again,' etc.

De Vries and Guttmann had done everything they possibly could to make the premiere a success. Rob had even set aside his ideal of cultural decentralization by opting for an opening night in the capital. Following the argument that a performance close to the real drama would be more than appropriate, the Amsterdam mayor pretty much claimed the premiere. At the very least, it would indeed made sense to feature the story of Anne Frank 'ten years after the war' in the same venue, the municipal theater, as *Free Folk*, all the more so because that liberation play had ignored the Shoah altogether. Due to a double booking, which caused a lot of stress and reproaches back and forth, part of the plan fell through. The ensemble had to move from the municipal theater to a less prestigious venue at the other side of the street. For some, this was yet another sign of the pettiness of the prevailing commemorative policy.

DOI: 10.4324/9781032034324-5

The De la Mar theater was located in a former school building that served as a storage for the municipal theater. After the war, facilities for a theater were installed with actress Fien de la Mar as manager. In the early 1950s, cabaret artist Wim Sonneveld took over the helm. After the performance, the actors paid their respects to the executed resistance fighters who tried to set fire to the archives of the German forced labor office that was once located in the structure. At 200 m from the theater stood the prison where a few cast members and the Frank family had been held.

The theater hall was relatively small with fewer than 400 seats and poor facilities, making it difficult to catch the diary fragments. The municipal theater had a tiered hall with a view on both the stage and fellow spectators. Instead, De la Mar was small and run down. The hall had 15 rows and there was a small balcony with an exclusive focus on the stage. Still, all things considered, it was fortunate that opening night was held in the capital and even on Leidseplein, one of the city's theater and nightlife centers. If the municipal theater was the stage for serious drama, then the adjacent Leidseplein Theater had the same significance for prewar cabaret: from Carl Tobi and his many talents, of which many had made their debut in the war (including Wim Sonneveld) and from the exile cabaret of Erika Mann and Kabaret Ping-Pong who, if only briefly, had triumphed at the same location.

The De la Mar theater was literally attached to the Americain, a huge fin-de-siècle art deco hotel whose café was Harry Mulisch's favorite spot. The writer had just moved into an apartment on a street behind the theater. There's another thing about the Americain: in Belsen, Margot and Anne had sought support from two sisters from the Weesperstraat in the Jewish quarter with whom they took turns telling stories. 'Mostly they were about food,' as one of them, Rebekka Brilleslijper, better known as Lin Jaldati, interpreter of Yiddish songs, remembered: 'Once we talked about going to the Americain for dinner. Anne suddenly burst into tears at the thought that we would never return.'[1] Retroactively, as a sort of off-Broadway theater and lieu de mémoire all in one, De la Mar appears to have been very appropriate, intimate and in keeping with the play's status, being neither fringe nor repertory drama. It kind of spiced up the premiere and the ensemble would return twice for longer periods.

The crowd poured in with many special guests among them: three of the best-known helpers – Miep Gies, Bep Voskuijl and Johannes Kleiman – survivors, colleagues and many critics. Voskuijl ran into 'Dirk, the vegetable man,' as mentioned in Scene 9, who belonged to the knowing of the secret annex and whom she had not seen in years.[2] Anne's best friend Jacqueline van Maarsen, in the diary known as Jopie, was also present.

Among the public were the Israeli ambassador, the Dutch Chief Rabbi and Queen Juliana. A royal box was missing and the usual floral decoration for her seat was omitted. The same was true of gala attire. The queen wore 'a simple black wool dress.'

The early birds were able to browse the program booklet, designed by graphic designer JF (Eppo) Doeve. The Dutch and German program notes differed from those of New York. Absent were the usual glamour photos and instead lyrics were included aligning the playscript with more recognizable Jewish texts. The German program notes included parts from the *Book of Lamentations*, lyrics from religious songs, background information on the poor postwar reception of survivors and a list of Jewish Nobel Prize laureates. Sometimes, like in Munich, a Christian redemption symbolism prevailed. Very interesting was the decision to include the two key diary quotes more extensively in the Dutch booklet. The first was the one from which Anne's aphorism had been adopted but which was more gloomy when read in full: 'I hear the ever-approaching thunder, which will destroy us too.' The second concerned the specific fate that had befallen the Jews: 'God has never forsaken our people. . . . Throughout the ages, Jews have suffered.' Karl Guttmann had added a short note in which he grouped Anne among 'the greatest of her people' and had a text printed on a portrait of Anne from the Midrash, an ancient biblical commentary, that translated Jewish suffering into empathy. *Let not strike you that which has struck me, let it not happen to you what happened to me.* Through the program notes, the ensemble thus made another crucial supplement to the script, priming audiences to the Jewishness and tone of the drama.

At the time, the curtain still fulfilled its traditional role in separating the world onstage from the world outside. It was certainly very present in this play because the curtain fell between all the scenes. The chime sounded three times and when everyone was seated, the lights went off and the velvet curtain was raised. The hidden world of the secret annex was revealed, the carillon of the Westertoren rang out, followed by the tunes of a barrel organ seeping through the walls from outside. In a way, it was a bit blunt to access the world of the annexants, when they themselves could only peek out from behind the tiny cracks in the shutters.

The set acted as a peep box into a hidden interior just as the diary functioned for Anne's musings. The stage was transformed into the interior of a canal house with a view of the outside façades and the bell tower of the Westerkerk. Boris Aronson's set design was slightly modified by Wim Vasseur (who would also assist Guttmann in Frankfurt), but the key elements were there: the bookcase, the bell tower, Anne's room with her little desk and the photo wall. Perhaps the set had fallen prey to Aronson's penchant for over-design, but it certainly helped draw spectators into the hideout's confined interior. So while the rooms in the secret annex were spread over two floors and an attic, onstage all of this was reduced to a single miniature open space with a few doors and windows. Spectators with an eye for detail will have noticed that the division of space between the two families was exactly the opposite of what it had been like. On stage, Otto and Edith slept in the kitchen instead of the Van Daans, which had the effect of marking a distinction between main and minor characters.

The set is another example of the crucial input of Jewish theater practitioners, adding that director Kanin and producer Kermit Bloomgarden were Jewish as well. Boris Aronson was one of ten children of a Kiev rabbi who came from a chain of rabbinic families. He became interested in the post-revolutionary wave of modernism at a young age and got involved in the world of painting and theater. This is when he published a book on the painter Marc Chagall. When the family moved to Tel Aviv, Boris went in the opposite direction, first to Berlin and then New York, designing for the prolific Yiddish theater. In 1945, he married Lisa Jalowetz who had studied set design in Reinhardt's Vienna but, as so many, fled, first to Amsterdam and just before the German invasion to the United States. Together, the Aronsons would create a series of famous postwar sets, building on both European experiences: Arthur Miller's *The Crucible*, *Cabaret* and *Fiddler on the Roof*.

In Europe, Aronson was under the spell of Expressionism, but on Broadway he had to meet the demand for realistic set interiors. One can only design so many realistic kitchen sinks and expressionism slowly trickled back in. It was then that *The Diary of Anne Frank* came his way. The design was seemingly realistic in layout and materiality and the textures of weathered wood and chipped plaster explain why Marc Aronson emphasized the tactility of his parents' designs. In its compactness and the perspectivist juxtaposition of inside and outside, it was the epitome of an expressionist imagination. The actors had little room for maneuver – as Anne-Marie Heyligers remembers very well – and that claustrophobic atmosphere was transferred to the audience, enhanced by the small premiere theater. Tight agreements had to be made about where to hide during the numerous prop changements. The set was realistic compared to the magical realism of the Fiddler-set that came straight out of a Chagall painting with its circular houses floating in mid-air, but in a way it exuded a similar fantasy-like atmosphere: as an invitation to visualize the dreams Anne wrote about and thus conceive of the theater space as a subjective representation of Anne's mind. But that expressionist allusion of Anne in Wonderland was not picked up.[3]

For the Dutch premiere audience, the soundscape was recognizable and imbued with meaning and affection. This was especially true for the carillon. Some recognized the soldier's song *Erika* from the occupation and singing the national anthem in celebration of the invasion in Scene 8 – not in the diary – will have been special in the presence of royalty. There were probably three reels, one for the chimes, one for Anne's voice and one for additional sounds plus additional manual sound effects, especially in the burglary scene and during the arrest.[4]

Assessing the acting remains delicate. Thanks to a fragment of a dialogue recorded the day before, I was able to present his younger self to Croiset. The actor has a characteristically deep voice and he was sometimes accused of overacting because of his resonant speech. Croiset noticed how the words need to be pronounced a little bit more naturally, as if you were making them up on the spot. As if there was no repetition, as if true life were taking place on stage and acting was discontinued. That was the way typecasting was intended and it seemed that Crefcoeur and Heyligers reached that point. It is a familiar condition of a character running away with the actor. And although she was more aloof than some of the others, Heyligers suffered from this condition right through the premiere. She felt herself completely absorbed in the role of Margot and it felt terrible: 'Anne-Marie was completely gone!' From now on, as she impressed upon herself, she had to rely on her acting skills if she wanted to make it through the series of performances in one piece. Crefcoeur had similar feelings of letting the play get too close, especially at the climax of the arrest. It took her a few shows to get adjusted. It will have been visible on opening night because she was complimented for her disarming and dedicated acting.[5]

Actor Bernhard Droog (Dussel) was known for his 'natural' acting, close to his own personality. He was typecast and that worked out completely. Rob, the *fearless lad*, was occasionally called upon to ham up his parts and that may explain the compliments for his controlled and modest acting style this time. In general, according to the critics, it was precisely the restraint and austerity in the acting – and subdued direction – that would make the production stand out, almost as a metaphor for the kind of commemorative sentiments the play prescribed.

The performance started quietly with Otto shuffling onto the stage of the dusty annex, grabbing the scarf – which Anne had given him for Hanukkah – and that was seen by one reviewer as a symbolic tallit.[6] Immediately afterward – for which Rob had to quickly change his appearance – the entry of the annexants introduced the coming to life of the annex. When the seven annexants had entered, with Peter holding on to the cat basket, spunky Anne made her stage entrance. Now the plot could unfold. A critical moment came with the Hanukkah scene that took place in the twilight and shadow of the burglary. It was a provisional evocative highlight, one with which the cast seemed to have already settled the score. Visitors could now relax in the lobby. The cast will not have been dissatisfied. During the dress rehearsal, they had already noticed that audience reactions were quite unusual; and opening night was no different. Although the play contained numerous funny situations, there was little to no laughter, as if the audience did not dare to show their enjoyment – and as if they had taken notice of Ies Spetter's horror at a laughing audience. However, sobs could be heard throughout the hall.

The part after the break was a roller-coaster of events and emotions. The mutual tensions increased – there was the theft of bread, but the hope for liberation also grew. Anne and Peter got more intimate and toward the end of the play, the annexants danced across the room when the invasion is announced. The end came suddenly and with a thunderous roar followed by 'one strangled cry' – that is, from the audience. With the arrest, two orange crates suggested that the lower doors were torn down. A sledge hammer and a plank would evoke the book case being shattered that made a frightening noise. The final sound effect was even more terrifying. A weight of 75 pounds fell from 5 m through a layer of boxes onto a metal trash can.[7] Blackout! We were back in the dusty postwar attic with Otto, morally cleansed from going through the diary, and ready to take in Anne's words one more time. Curtain.

Figure 9 Karl Guttmann and Rob de Vries receive the queen's congratulations (S. van Collem/Archive Karl Guttmann)

The final curtain was not followed by the usual curtain call. Silence reigned, sobs could still be heard but no applause. Nobody got up. After a few minutes, the royal party left the hall. The queen was seen with tears in her eyes. Now the remaining audience started shuffling toward the exit too. Here and there people gently exchanged a few words. When the hall was almost empty, Rika Hopper, 'the queen of Dutch theater,' who had had her farewell performance with the ensemble of De Vries, passed the row of helpers. Shaking her head and barely controlling her emotions, she called out to them: 'What a drama, what a play. How is it possible that such a thing could happen in this day and age. Alas, it really happened.'[8] After the show, in the lobby, Karl and Rob were congratulated by the royal guests, the three helpers and others if they managed to get near in the bustle. Ms. Voskuijl shook hands with Rob, but could not utter a single word, only later did she express her gratitude and told him how identical the three young actors were with the real Anne, Margot and Peter.[9] Some would later apologize for having left hurriedly because of the excitement or because of their tears. They left the theater and immediately found themselves in the hustle and bustle of Amsterdam's traffic and nightlife.

No applause

The lack of applause became a hallmark of the premiere. The omission was not just an absence of sound, but an atmosphere of silence, a meaningful 'burdensome silence,' a 'sacred silence . . . the only right thing to do in the circumstances,' a silence 'out of respect for the tragedy of the Amsterdam Jewish girl,' arguably also an incriminating silence.[10] Audience behavior at the premiere became the standard and so two months later in Rotterdam, people shuffled through the aisles in 'silent afflicted poignancy' and the same was true of The Hague:

> The curtain fell and the group of immobilized spectators slowly became themselves. . . . I saw the audience through a peephole in the curtain. . . . They left as if they had been given a beating. 'No applause,' someone shouted backstage, 'lower the screen!'

The omission of applause was urgent enough for Rob to report Otto about the 'wonderful' audience responses. 'There's very seldom applause. But the letters I receive are piling up.'[11] Correspondents cited the lack of applause as the main reason for expressing their appreciation by mail, because, as one correspondent put it, 'I was unable to express my appreciation in the usual somewhat noisy way.' A second correspondent thought it was the only right thing to do and a third stated 'that we were afraid to applaud.' One correspondent was dissatisfied because for the actor it maybe 'more satisfying than a splashing applause,' the spectator still yearns for his 'act of relief.' Theatrical lore has it that there was a call in the lobby to refrain from applause. There is no evidence for this and it was also flatly denied by Guttmann who pointed out that the cast was 'actually waiting in the wings but when there was no applause, I decided to leave it at that.'[12]

There was some applause though, not at the premiere but during the tour. So not everyone followed the unwritten code of conduct. Six weeks after the premiere, people in Rotterdam sniffled and applauded 'albeit without conviction.' According to the reviewer, a noted writer, this concerned the 'uncivilized part of the audience' and their behavior was 'quickly suppressed.' In any case, there was too much noise, coughing and grumbling, 'an inadequate reception . . . worse than disturbing, painful.' Let's hope later shows will have 'a more appropriate atmosphere.'[13] In agreement with Otto onstage, and like the Drenthe governor (see Chapter 1), one reviewer explained his silence in terms of shame, 'because we feel guilty as a generation.'[14]

The practice followed upon the German shows. Critic Tynan had already written about how German visitors left the building with heads bowed down in total silence. His observation was included in the Dutch press publicity. But again it was a matter of one part of the audience disciplining the other. The Berlin audience 'left the theater in dismay. A weak applause from a few was suppressed in the overall silence, which turned out to be the only appropriate answer after the performance.' The show didn't end with the final curtain, but entered the private sphere. The silence 'was carried along in the tram from Stieglitz, driving back to the center of Berlin. We sat in the midst of silent passengers who brought the show home.' Months later, Karl Guttmann achieved a minute-long silent triumph in Frankfurt, but again there were 'timid attempts at applause.'[15] There was one big difference, however. In Germany, some program notes urged spectators to refrain from acclamation: '*Es wird gebeten, von Beifallsaüsserungen abzusehen.*'[16]

The absence of applause made up for the performances' designation as a mourning ritual, as Karl and others did. After all, you wouldn't applaud after a poignant funeral speech either. It does explain the sentiment of grief that lingered after the show. Still, despite the resemblances, the omission of applause was a performative act that was mainly to be understood within the confines of the theater. It was the audience's contribution after the actors' deliverance in the preceding two hours. It was an act that had been prepared, possibly prescribed, but of which it was always uncertain whether it would happen as planned.

What exactly happens in an auditorium when thinking of individual visitors and the audience as a collective? Should we assume that the lack of applause signalled a similar emotion among spectators – with different backgrounds – or perhaps that somehow this emotion jumped from one to the other as suggested in the notion of affective contagion? It might be better to consider how in the practice of (the lack of) applause the theater audience, the self and the other took shape. And thus allow the notion of empathy as a bond between self and the other to have effect. Empathy could be attached to the signs – the elements that make up the play, including characters and actors – in the moment of the performance. But a history of involvement with the diary, the actors and the theater, and the war past preceded this. The public involvement might have included reading the diary, anticipating how the book publication would have been turned into a theatrical adaptation, the buzz surrounding the upcoming premiere – which already caused requests for tickets to flow in, the choice of clothing and the entrance to the auditorium. Audiences were informed by the program notes and in later shows potential spectators were able to obtain information from the reviews. Anne Frank – as a historical person, as the author of a diary, as a character on stage – acted as a flywheel for this empathic process, but with the specification that she herself emerged as an object of empathy in this drawn-out process.[17]

Catharsis

The helpers were deeply impressed from the start. Miep Gies immediately had a difficult time in the first scene in which Otto receives the diary from her stage version and she 'barely made it to the end.' The play reverberated in Kleiman's mind and it took him days to part with it. Bep Voskuijl 'got the worst of it when the Grünen knocked on the door and just as on August 4, 1944, she burst into sobs and trembled with misery.'[18] Jacqueline van Maarsen sat incognito in the hall, but when the name of 'Jopie' came up, she and her husband looked each other in the eye. She very much appreciated the gesture with the scarf in Scene 1, even though 'it wasn't Anne on stage.' The program booklet became the first piece in her Anne Frank collection.[19]

There were survivors – that is, people who disclosed their background in these terms – that attended the show and whom were caught by the play. 'I will remember the performance for a long time.' There was 'an open wound,' after having spent two years in Belsen, but even more so 'I am grateful for your courage and energy to stage this play.'[20] This must have been encouraging for Rob and Karl after the preliminary negative survivor responses. A second survivor – who had followed the same trajectory as Anne – fleeing from Germany to Holland, into hiding, being arrested, Westerbork, Belsen – complimented the cast: 'I've never seen anything that had felt so right.' The performance brought back a traumatic past for the comedian and theater producer Carl Tobi and that became too much: 'You let your thoughts go back to that terrible time . . . and then all these images float to the surface . . . and then you experience everything once more.' Tobi made his apologies for rushing home after the performance, he simply could not cope with his memories: and to think of it that 'I will soon be working on the outdoor shoot of the Fox film 'The Diary of Anne Frank.' I'll get to relive everything that you luckily left out.'[21] The 'events' onstage made the personal past manifest.

These were individual responses, some of which we might group, such as was done here. But there was also a social dynamic in the hall. There might be silence afterward, yet all kinds of things happened during the show. Kleiman noticed a 'tension' in the hall, a collective affection, sensing, as he added, that people were caught. It seems that the audience was not only subjected to discipline but also responded affectively, perhaps unintentionally, to what happened on stage and in the theater hall. Aside from the ending, the Hanukkah scene just before the intermission sparked a particular emotional 'outburst.' Croiset claims to recall that spectators responded violently to the scene and that meant that people could pass out too: 'During the intermission, people were led away through the artist's entrance – on stretchers, if necessary – so as not to disturb the people in the theater.'

Looking back 30 years later, Karl Guttmann came up with the drama term catharsis to indicate the impact. The term was in use at the time. Just think of Tynan's experiences during the Berlin performance when the critic 'tried hard to stay detached' but was 'engulfed' by 'the general catharsis.' Perhaps that's what Crefcoeur meant when she observed how 'emotions lay heavy and tangible across the auditorium.'[22] There is the municipal theater's manager who had to cry but was 'not ashamed.' He couldn't reach Rob in the lobby, but he was able to embrace Rob's wife. In other words, there was a bodily activity of crying that is comparable to Voskuijl's 'trembling' and then an embrace. The manager added that his extensive knowledge and experience with the tricks of the actor's trade had failed him for once. On stage Rob and Otto appeared identical.

It is not surprising that so many brought up the term catharsis as it is a familiar concept in drama theory. In his *Poetics*, Aristotle gave little clarification, which led to centuries of interpretation, ranging from catharsis as (ritual) purification of morals – that is, theater as a pathway to moral virtue (for which Drenthe's governor is an apt example), which might have been Rob's objective all along – to healing of a supposed ailment of the affect, as picked up by Sigmund Freud: theater as a stage for pent-up emotions.[23]

In the latter instance, catharsis describes the sudden confrontation with elements of a traumatic memory. Freud, whose psychoanalysis owed much to his familiarity with ancient Greek drama, postulated that anomalous experiences can have such an affective impact that they do not acquire an orderly place in man's emotional balance sheet.[24] They remain latent, their meaning is deferred and manifest in ways beyond conscious human control, either in speech (for example, through jokes) or in imaginings (through dreams). The theater is such a privileged platform where deferred past events become manifest and the unconscious comes to the surface: wrapped in an artistic form, but therefore completely revealing. In the theater, repression finds an acceptable form of expression.[25] The notion of repression implies a parting of affect and past event. Here onstage in the singularity of the play, they were brought back together again. The act of conjuring up a past never is flawless however and the staging therefore offers something new – like a possible alignment with signs put onstage. Occasionally, the play acting as a vehicle for mixing different pasts became very tangible. One friend from the Resistance literally mistook Rob in his impersonation as Otto for a mutual deceased friend from the Resistance, and therefore 'this play also tells something about the suffering' of our friends 'in a small basement on the Keizersgracht.'[26] It was as if the attic with its scattered objects and with Anne symbolically eternally locked up in the annex had become the storage space for all those ghostly memories. Achieving this effect can be attributed to a well-made play that sticks. It must be everything that Rob de Vries had hoped for.

Catharsis assumes a stirring of the passions – the arousal of fear and pity – through empathy with the actors and characters onstage, and that is detectible in some of the public responses. The play was not necessarily the starting point. There was already a circulation of signs in operation before people entered the auditorium. The play brought together a number of elements in a proposal to view the past priming and prompting spectators to identify. There's also a more vague effusion indicating that the affect was open-ended, not always filled in by distinctive indexable emotions but rather a combined physical and mental response to the events on and around the stage. The affect was perceived as unsettling, aligned to a source – the events as signs onstage – but not necessarily working toward a well-defined objective. Theater digs from the depths exposing 'hidden layers of memory' that transport the body 'into a hitherto unknown state,' as historian Aleida Assmann put it.[27] Several responses referred to a punch in the stomach. The Dutch words used have a similar tactile connotation, such as being touched and being caught. There were trembling and paralyzed bodies, throbbing hearts, dry lips, soggy eyes and searing throats. These physical responses may be accounted for as an experience of loss of physical and mental control and of distress in realizing that 'the Ego is not master in its own house.'[28]

Distinctive audiences, distinctive responses

Theater as an accepted art form is closely linked to unwritten codes of conduct and evaluations. For some, refraining from applause was bound up with a distinct sensibility necessary to perceive and appreciate art. In one town, the corrupt 'theater habits' of 'one part of the audience' made it impossible for 'the majority' to fully concentrate, whereas precisely this play commands 'extreme ardor and mental effort.' There were counter-voices: 'Don't hiss but give people the chance to respond in their own particular way. After all, it still is theater.'[29] In general, however, critics not only described the practice as it unfolded, but also informed and prescribed the rules of conduct for future audiences. But these markings of distinction went further.

The emotions the play sought to arouse stemmed from commercialism that went against the grain of respectable drama, as was said. What made Broadway so exciting from an Amsterdam perspective – the cut throat battle for commercial success – got in the way of appreciation when seen from the Dutch subsidized theatrical field. The play was not primarily appreciated as an artistic work of art. The Jewish Weekly spoke of a *Broadway Schlager*, a lachrymose tearjerker.[30] Melodrama is the usual derogatory term for a performance with an excess of pity.

Some critics' responses highlight a certain affective disposition and a disregard for the craft needed to create an emotionally effective play. One literary critic was deeply moved, but he was very suspicious of his own corporeal reactions. His strong emotions had nothing to do with the 'vulgar play' but should be attributed to the 'historical events,' or so he argued. The dramatists were too 'mentally lazy' to turn history into art. Perhaps this author showed his true colors when he simultaneously began tearing down the diary as 'clumsy inflated teenage prose.'[31] Harry Mulisch – who was busy starting out as a playwright and theater critic, and who didn't find it necessary to read the diary – reacted similarly:

> It was the most awful experience I've ever had in a theater. Unprocessed and hardly artistic, it punched me in the gut. . . . I don't think such an experience belongs in a theater and I left the auditorium devastated. It was anathema to see this misery, so real, so direct.[32]

Note the violence that accompanied his theatrical experience. A play that hands the spectators a sucker punch. 'Mission accomplished,' you would think if you were in De Vries's shoes. Both critics averted the input of theater and responded as if the past came to them unmediated. Mulisch furthermore acknowledged he was affected, even overwhelmed and immersed in a collective of spectators, but he didn't see this in positive terms, nor did he seem able to work out his feelings. What was clever about Tynan's observation was that he recognized the paradox: how one can be affected by enjoyment and still experience aversion: 'I can only record an emotion that I felt, would not have missed and pray to never feel again.' Of course, this opening up of unthought-of sources of pleasure had long been pointed out by Freud when he noted that the artistic play 'does not spare the spectators most painful experiences and can yet be felt by them as highly enjoyable.'[33]

Gomperts was one of those critics who rejected the playscript for its commercially induced emotional effects. Yet the critic gave himself and the production a second chance. One day after the premiere, he declared he had succumbed to the general catharsis.

> This was not a drama, not an imagination, but terrible reality itself. I must confess that I have never experienced such a great and massive emotion in a theater before. . . . Visit the play if your nerves can withstand the emotions.

Critic Gomperts still believed that the Hacketts had sought 'dramatic effect' at the expense of Anne's 'austere writing,' but what he had underestimated was the force with which the performance pressed upon his mood. The diary remained superior, but the dramatic effect of the Hanukkah celebration hit harder. Influenced by his own, unspecified, war memories – he was Jewish and had fled to London in 1940, his father had been a member of the Jewish Council – Gomperts had experienced the ending of the play 'as an unbearable pain.' He was thus (!) thrilled that his 'wish at the time to put the play aside had not been fulfilled.'

As on Broadway, the ensemble's goal was to attract as many audiences as possible. But the motivational background was different. Here it arose from De Vries's strong support for the policy of cultural dissemination and from Otto's efforts to spread Anne's 'message.' The former peat cutters of Emmen had to be reached too. The introduction of a school program was consistent with this ideal. It had been a promise from Rob from long before the premiere. The pupils were certainly among the ordinary spectators who, unlike critics, were not bound by the conventional rubrics for reviewing. Crefcoeur noticed they liked the jokes and laughed out loud, unlike the adults who would hardly ever allow themselves to express their pleasure, except occasionally when they laughed 'nervously at their own reflection' as she diagnosed like a modern-day Freud.[34]

Rob had asked for reactions and so he received essays, for example, from a school in Haarlem.[35] From the current day and age, it's striking that these young people who lived through the war – which they will have propagated in later life – stressed their lack of knowledge and experience. Occasionally, there was a strong identification with Anne or Peter. One student had been to the show twice and cried on both occasions.

> We know so little about the war; I was born in 1940. When the adults talk about it, we listen without understanding. . . . I was captivated by the play and have come to love Anne Frank. She stayed with me the following days at school. . . . I kept catching myself thinking about her.

This was the type of response Otto had grown accustomed to since the diary was published. Croiset received a letter addressing him as Peter. The performance was a highlight in the young correspondent's life. Of all the actors, 'you' made the biggest impression. 'I recognized myself in you. . . . [T]here is a vague similarity . . . you have given me something that I will be grateful for all my life. . . . Sorry to call you Peter.'[36] Empathy, as we have already seen, follows the route of the stage and may stick to the relationship between spectator and actor. More identifications were reported: 'You were not an actor, you were "the father" ' and: 'Anne was seen on stage instead of some actress!'[37]

A pupil had lived through the war but confessed she 'would never sense what people who truly lived through those times consciously felt about such stories.' When reading the diary, 'the only thing that remains is the surprise that the things she wrote down could be so completely related to yourself.' However, the play was disappointing because there was little left of the emotional excitement of reading certain events in the book. Unlike the play, the book made her cry every time she read it. Disappointment of the adaptation also characterized the astute reading of another student. First she complimented Crefcoeur and Croiset (who 'had a wonderful sense of the temperament of such an adolescent kid') while expressing her cultural competence to assess the show. She was an experienced theater visitor. Dussel was an exaggeration: 'From the book I did not portray him as such an unsympathetic man,' a discrepancy that was never noticed in official reviews. 'De Vries started overacting but got better over time.' But overall it was still disappointing:

> I often have days to doze over a good play or a good book, but as soon as I left the De la Mar theater I had forgotten the whole thing. And I was not alone, many of my classmates felt the same way.

Would it be due to the distance in time, but no, the diary had made a big impression: 'This was, in short, my assessment of your performance. I hope you don't find me very ungrateful.'[38]

On tour

The premiere successfully marked the end of a long adventure that Rob de Vries embarked upon two years before. The weight of the moment had certainly not escaped him. 'How often does an artist experience such a time? Until now . . . only once,' as he impressed upon Guttmann, who had already moved on to Frankfurt and Vienna, 'and that was largely because of you. It was a great time. Thank you Karl.'[39] Guttmann would agree because he counted it as one of the three highlights of his life, along with the return to Bielitz and the declaration of the State of Israel. On opening night, Otto had thanked the cast for their dedication, wishing that the audience 'be influenced for the better and the play elicits a better understanding among mankind.' Rob in turn, and fresh on, disclosed that the premiere as well as the performances were part of the greatest event in his acting career. 'I am very grateful that we persisted in spite of gloomy predictions.' Following upon his earlier account, he reported that 'the entire ensemble acts with great dedication every night,' assuring Otto the main target still was to show the play in the entire country, 'so that the message is heard and understood without any restrictions. That makes me joyful and I hope you too.'

Hidden in Karl's carton boxes was a small card to be attached to a bouquet of flowers. *Martine Crefcoeur. De la Mar Theater. From Mom and Dad.* The moment of opening night was prodigious, from drama school into the spotlights. For Jules Croiset and Anne-Marie Heyligers, despite her skepticism, the moment will also have been special. Croiset received a 'Go get them!' telegram from his brother Hans and a good luck card from his parents.

Despite the hustle and bustle of the premiere, it is also just the first performance and perhaps not the most representative in that regard. It took Rob little time to fully capture the enormity of the event and the need for the ensemble to go along with it. The ensemble program was rearranged in a way that the play was given as much room as possible. Enny Mols was bought free from her engagement with the radio broadcaster, Crefcoeur was accommodated in her complicated school and performance schedule. Jules Croiset would move to The Hague at the end of the 1956–1957 season, Huib de Vries (no relation) being his substitute in the second season. Heyligers would complete the series to the end. Only when the play was televised in

1962 did she wholeheartedly refuse to join the production, much to Karl's utter astonishment. Kitty Courbois who was at the start of an impressive career was to be her replacement.[40]

The play caught on as Rob kept on reporting to Otto: the unstoppable enthusiasm, the requests for tickets, the people queuing at 6 a.m., even bringing their own folding chairs: 'We have not experienced anything like this after the war. . . . It's really all incredible.' Yet he never lost sight of the solemn attitude: 'But the crazy thing about it is that my personal success does much less to me than the fact that so many people experience the past again and do not forget about it.' This must be what Rob meant when he spoke of his urge to blow the whistle once a year, after his relentless struggle during the war, being part of the resistance, and being imprisoned, with his family in hiding, losing friends and colleagues. The same feeling must have lived with Karl: associated with theater from an early age in a country that no longer existed, persecuted and emigrated to a country that would become a nation, to end up in the Netherlands. In the spring of 1957, Karl obtained his Dutch citizenship. Chased from Vienna, he would return as the director of a play about this very persecution. That wasn't for everyone. The Dutch cast sent a good luck telegram to Vienna, adding that all their success had been 'dependent' upon Guttmann's efforts.

After the first series of Amsterdam performances, the ensemble traveled through the country, with stories about the play's relevance and prescribed audience behavior rushing them ahead. A balance had to be found between deepening a role, routine and the singularity of the performance. Crefcoeur was still tinkering with her part, working toward the moment when the intensity on stage could be exchanged for a relaxed cup of coffee backstage, but in these first few weeks she also discovered the 'endless variations' that lie in pronunciation and tone and 'in the way you can be someone' onstage.

The enthusiasm continued to be breathtaking, the tour was both unique and exhausting and Otto remained quite demanding. When Rob spoke about the overall positive response he encountered, Otto replied that the intention must be to reach the farthest corners of the country.[41] It was too easy to be successful only in the urban west. And indeed people often missed out: 'For once we from the countryside would like to attend a performance as well, but we see no chance to do so because the seats are already taken before the official sale starts.'

In the first season – between November 1956 and September 1957 – there were 175 performances crisscrossing the country, leading up to at least 240. Jules Croiset noted, tongue in cheek, that every so often an attempt is made to organize a tour according to some topographical logic.

But in vain. The playlist does show some logic though. Even better was the period in mid-April–May 1957, when the company spent a month in Amsterdam in De la Mar. The hall had been renovated in the meantime, allowing for more spectators. That period will have given the cast some relief. On tour in the 1950s meant narrow roads, especially in the province, many dual carriageways, in a bus that was either too cold or too stuffy.[42] It took a lot of time alone to pick up cast members at home. The actors left before 5 p.m. with pocket money to dine on site. Sometimes there were two performances in a day, a matinee and an evening performance. The actors then left in the morning, played at 2 p.m. and again at 8 p.m. They might stay overnight and move on the next day. Usually they returned home at 1 o'clock in the morning. Of course, this was every actors life yet the pace was special for the Netherlands. And then at a certain point, the rut snuck in. The production was accompanied by a special tension, not just for the spectators. According to Croiset, they were not allowed to have fun on the road, and playing cards was also prohibited.[43] A serene atmosphere also had to be observed in the bus.

The actors had to cope with the audience responses, with the lack of applause as most typical feature. Heyligers didn't remember ever having a round of applause. 'The lights went out and the hall emptied. The curtain just fell.' Jules Croiset could 'still hear the silence on stage' while waiting for people to get up after the show and then leave the stage. 'People didn't applaud anywhere. And that was awful.' Looking back, Crefcoeur rather pointed to an opposite response among cast members: 'Sometimes people would applaud because spectators crave an outlet for their emotions and then I noticed that the cast wouldn't appreciate that' because it broke the anticipated atmosphere.[44]

The actors could perform routinely and with craftsmanship, especially because of the high frequency, but there was still, or maybe because of that, a stiff atmosphere. That tension sometimes would receive an uncomfortable exhaust valve, such as in a theater where the dignified atmosphere of the Hanukkah ritual was broken when the players got the giggles and couldn't stop. The curtain was quickly dropped after which they were scolded by Rob backstage. At another occasion, the distribution of the potatoes went wrong. The stage directions prescribed that the potatoes were to be boiled first to prevent hem from rolling. That went wrong once and when Dussel could not hold them, everyone burst out laughing. Heyligers: 'We were "full back" but the spectators were so conditioned that they assumed we were crying.' At another occasion, as Croiset recalls, Mouschi the cat – what were the Hacketts thinking about including a live animal onstage – went missing. Another and truly low point for Heyligers was an incident at the Hanukkah dinner. Anne and Margot shared the food – a mixture of apple and pineapple – around the table. The first being served was Mrs. Van Daan. 'That's how we went around and the last was Martine and me. I had not realized that, but at a certain point it turned out that we had more pineapple on our plate than apple. That had not dawned on me. Until one point, Enny Mols started complaining. She said, "Guys, you do it on purpose." "Huh? I'm just serving. Martine and I were not aware of any malicious intent." When there was another similar complaint afterward, "I truly had enough of it." '

After six months, the ensemble returned to Amsterdam. On May 4, on the National Day of Remembrance, they would perform – this time in the municipal theater – and be present at the wreath-laying ceremony. The cast should queue up at a prescribed location on Dam Square but the three actors in the roles of Anne, Margot and Peter felt uncomfortable and refused to comply. The performance that evening ended at 12:30 a.m. and, as usual, in silence. This time the effect was that of a second two minutes of silence after the 8 o'clock commemorative silence.

The evenings were concluded with a follow-up backstage. In Dutch this was the *na-zit*, but in this play one collaborator jokingly had come up with the *na-snik*, the after-sob, because of the regular emotional blow off. The joke allowed for mockery and showed awareness of the peculiar circumstances they found themselves, night after night. February 1957, the Hacketts stopped by at one of those backstage *after-sobs* to say thanks and point out how happy they were with the success. Guttmann received a signed copy of the script.

After some time, the grind was broken for some: 'Fatigue, the concentration disappears, because it was not all that interesting what we had to do there, really not. I know because I sat listening to it night after night.' Heyligers was professional enough to deal with this:

> You must continue to focus on what is expected of you. . . . I don't know if we were fully featured, but anyway you were all the time present onstage. You should never forget that. I did notice that sometimes my thoughts were elsewhere. . . . Still, everyone could look at you, you couldn't just start picking your nose.

Heyligers was happy when she simultaneously had to act in another play. It alleviated her presence in a play that she did not like in the first place and in which she hardly had any lines. It would of course be great if we had access to the memories of her fellow cast members. It got more difficult for Rob de Vries. His job as ensemble manager remained demanding.

He sometimes stood on the stage tired, as he confessed to Otto: 'It is truly exhausting to play so intensively in this play night after night, but I do it with all my heart.' At one point, as Heyligers remembers, 'we noticed that he no longer had any concentration left, not knowing his lines and almost asleep on stage.' Rob also had visible health problems now and then, even on stage, but he quickly dismissed these when colleagues showed their concerns.

In 1957, a failed attempt had already been made to get the show on television. In 1962, it went ahead provided the recordings were destroyed. Earlier in the week, Rob came to tell about the great escape from Westerbork on television. In that same year, Harry Mulisch made another unsuccessful attempt to revive his novel *The Future of Yesterday* – a what-if history of Nazi Germany winning the war, on which he had been working since 1956. In the non-fiction text that was left of it, he typically solipsistic concluded that when he began writing on the war, no one was interested in WWII. Three years later, when his *The Stone Bridal Bed* appeared, this had already somewhat changed.[45] In 1962, partly due to the Eichmann trial held in a theater hall, and his journalistic report, interest came to a tentative culmination. For the sake of convenience, the author forgot about the impact of the Anne Frank play.

Notes

1 Barry Denenberg, 'Fellow prisoners at Bergen-Belsen describe Anne Frank's last days,' in *Genocide in Anne Frank's the diary of a young girl*, ed. Louise Hawker (Detroit, 2012), 38–45, 41.
2 Joop van Wijk and Jeroen de Bruyn, *Anne Frank: The untold story; the hidden truth about Ellie Vossen, the youngest helper in the Secret Annex* (Laag-Soeren, 2018).
3 Details in: Alisa Solomon, *Wonder of wonders: A cultural history of Fiddler on the roof* (New York, 2014), 160; Marc Aronson Oral History Interview, by Christa Whitney, Yiddish Book Center's Wexler Oral History Project, Nyack, New York, May 23, 2016 via www.archive.org (accessed December 6, 2020); Sarah H. Lichtman, 'The diary of Anne Frank: Staging the secret annex and designs for an adolescent interior,' *Interiors* 10, 1–2 (2019): 123–151.
4 The audio reel with the Dutch diary excerpts has not been preserved, but there is still an English reel (KG Archive) that was used in a special performance in Frankfurt (January 28, 1957).
5 *Het Parool*, November 28, 1956.
6 *Haagsche Courant*, February 5, 1957.
7 As prescribed in the stage directions.
8 *The New York Times*, November 29, 1956; GA 0644, 183: Kleiman to De Vries.
9 UvA: Brvosku01, Voskuijl to De Vries, December 3, 1956.
10 Three reviews – one from *Het Parool* – included in Jules Croiset's scrapbook.

11 GA 0644, 183: De Vries to Frank, January 22, 1957.
12 UvA: E. de Vreede to De Vries, December 14, 1956; J. Eikenberg Spekman to Ensemble Theater, December 2, 1956; Brdek0001, Family Dekker to De Vries, January 13, 1957; GA 0644, 183: J. Houthakker to De Vries, May 5, 1957.
13 *Vrije Volk*, January 14, 1957; *Rotterdamsch Parool*, January 14, 1957.
14 *Alkmaarsche Courant*, January 7, 1957.
15 *Algemeen Handelsblad*, October 1956.
16 *Neue Presse*, January 21, 1957. For example, in Hannover and Düsseldorf. I was able to check the program notes of Dresden (East Germany), Konstanz, Münich, Köln, Düsseldorf, Frankfurt and Zürich (Switzerland).
17 In terms derived from Sara Ahmed, *The cultural politics of emotion* (Edinburgh, 2004), 10–13.
18 GA 0644, 183: Kleiman to De Vries, December 2, 1956.
19 Jacqueline van Maarsen, *Anne en Jopie. Leven met Anne Frank* (Amsterdam, 1990), 81.
20 UvA: G. van Hes-Perels to De Vries, December 2, 1956; Uva: Brsal001, Käthe Leffmann-Salinger to De Vries, November 25, 1956 (attending the play in Arnhem).
21 UvA: Brtobie02, Carl Tobi to De Vries, May 28, 1957.
22 *Het Parool*, February 14, 1984.
23 Aristotle, *Poëtica*, translated (into Dutch) and introduced by N. van der Ben and J.M. Bremer (Amsterdam, 1999), 186–187.
24 Favio Stok, 'Sigmund Freud's experience with the classics,' *Classica (Brasil)* 24, 1–2 (2011): 57–72.
25 On Freud's writings on catharsis, see: Jean-Michel Vives, 'Catharsis: Pyschoanalysis and the theatre,' *International Journal of Psychoanalysis* 92, 4 (2011): 1009–1027.
26 UvA: Brlind 001-1, Nelly Lind to De Vries, January 27, 1957.
27 Aleida Assmann, *Cultural memory and Western civilization: Functions, media, archives* (Cambridge, 2011), 152 (citing Proust).
28 Sigmund Freud, 'A difficulty in the path of psycho-analysis (1917),' *International Journal of Psycho-Analysis* 1 (1920): 17–23, First English publication.
29 *Nieuwe Tilburgse courant*, June 6, 1957; *Limburgs Nieuwsblad*, December 10, 1956.
30 *NIW*, December 12, 1956.
31 K. Greshoff, 'Het dagboek van Anne Frank. Aantekeningen bij het toneelstuk,' *Kroniek van Kunst en Kultuur* 17 (1958): 56–57.
32 *De Telegraaf*, May 4, 1962.
33 Sigmund Freud, *Beyond the pleasure principle* (New York and London, 1961), 17.
34 *Limburgs Dagblad*, January 9, 1957.
35 GA 0644, 183: Th. Ruygrok to De Vries, Bloemendaal, March 19, 1957.
36 Scrapbook Jules Croiset: D. van Willigen to J. Croiset, March 25, 1957.
37 UvA: Brkul0001, K.J. Kulb to De Vries, December 1, 1956.
38 GA 0644, 183: Greetje Filders to De Vries (no date); Liesbeth, F. to De Vries, May 30, 1957; Wilna Dekker to De Vries, May 30, 1957.
39 UvA: Brsali002, De Vries aan Guttmann (no date).
40 John de Freese, who played Mr Kraler, was killed in a tragic accident. His part was taken up by Jacques Snoek.
41 UvA, Brfr03, Frank to De Vries, April 1, 1957.
42 GA 0644: 16: Van Iersel to De Vries, October 11, 1953.

43 *Algemeen Dagblad*, February 4, 1984.
44 B&G: radio show *De stand van zaken*, December 2, 1983; *Haagsche Courant*, January 23, 1995.
45 Harry Mulisch, *De toekomst van gisteren: Protocol van een schrijverij* (Amsterdam, 1983), 56–60.

Figure 10 Weesperstraat, 1952, before the thoroughfare. The narrow street – crossed by the Lepelstraat – leads to the main artery of the Jewish quarter. The Jewish Secondary was situated on a side street (Stadsarchief Amsterdam)

Figure 11 Weesperstraat, 1976, with the thoroughfare, at the time of the construction of the metro. The roof below left-hand corner signals the access to the street of the Jewish Secondary (Stadsarchief Amsterdam)

5 Shibbolet

Postwar Jewishness onstage

Dear Rob, . . . The Hanukkah Celebration was too Protestant and neat for my taste.

–Wim Sonneveld, artist and manager

'A Holocaust Jew'

May 1957, the play opened in Vienna under the direction of Karl Guttmann, four days after the special Amsterdam performance on May 4. In the preceding months, Rob de Vries had quickly developed into an emissary of commemoration. Around May 4, he was invited to open an exposition at the Jewish Museum. Exhibits from three centuries of Jewish presence in the Netherlands, including documents relating to Anne's diary, offered the opportunity to regard the once thriving Jewish community through 'a haze of romance . . . before the big disaster.' A second exposition zoomed in on the demolition of the Jewish quarter. Plans for the large-scale renovation of the quarter had been announced a few months before and a model of the thoroughfare was part of the expo.[1] The actual execution of this urban renewal plan took a ten-year process to completion. The exhibits aligned the shards of a Jewish past with the erasure of the Jewish quarter in a mix of feelings of loss and modernization frenzy.

In the previous pages, the staging of *The Diary of Anne Frank* was presented as an eventful postwar history. Rob de Vries and Karl Guttmann had made a serious effort to stage a play that would 'blow the whistle' and manifest the absent presence of the Shoah in Dutch society. By aligning 'the war' and 'the occupation' with a Jewish experience of persecution, they hoped to instill sensitivity and empathy for the plight of European Jewry. The production was a collective venture and a personal victory, a watershed indeed. This was when Anne emerged as a personification of the Holocaust Jew, that is, an identification of Jews 'only in relation to Holocaust suffering' and Jewishness manifested through her apparition. Or, as critics claimed, Shoah

DOI: 10.4324/9781032034324-6

and Jewishness reduced to some kind of cheerful victimization.[2] Because a watershed suggests a simultaneous split and merging, it might be better to speak of an old trope in a new guise. After all, what was original about a theater of destruction since the tradition of purim spiels and the emergence of late nineteenth-century Jewish theater such as Herman Heijermans's one-act play *Ahasverus* (1893) on the Russian pogroms or Israel Zangwill's *The Melting Pot* (1908) referring to the Kishinev pogrom?

The Anne Frank play did not meet an empty stage. In fact, the play was depicted as 'a modern-day Heijermans.'[3] The world of drama was occupied by signs that set the stage for Rob and Karl's collective effort. First, words and signs such as war and occupation were already persuasively linked to sentiments of heroism and national mourning. Second, there was a Jewish literature of destruction to draw upon. Finally, on stage, persecution and Jewishness were already affectively aligned in different ways, even if more implicitly, with Jewish stock characters or with melancholy and nostalgia. A closer look at the involvement with some of these theatrical traces on the postwar stage reveals wide-ranging exchanges between different theatrical forms to manifest post-Shoah Jewishness.

Staging the ghetto

Jews returning in the summer of 1945 faced deep anxieties. The abandoned Jewish quarter looked desolate, leading to feelings of anger and grief. The mourning extended to the houses that had lost their souls and their right to exist in the absence of their inhabitants. Survivors must have experienced similar feelings of alienation as Otto Frank in the opening scene of the play, picking up at most some relics from the floor. The residents had been deported, the houses had been looted and stripped of useful materials, but many residential blocks were still standing. It had happened before. After WWI, the worst tenements had been cleared, the rest would follow in due course. Writer Siegfried van Praag saw the ruined ghetto as part of a centuries-long history of exile, destruction and persecution. Not only was the Temple in ashes, this time even the ghetto had to let go, the place where people had managed to build a new life in exile. The Jews were back to square one. Jewish experiences in the urban desert followed upon the notoriously poor reception after their return from the camps and hideouts: encountering indifference and antisemitism – properties not reimbursed while being charged with back taxes by numb bureaucracies. Many returnees did not have a Miep Gies waiting for them. All this added up to their trauma.

Mourning is a process of the gradual recognition of the inevitable: there is no going back to the past, the fissure is permanent, the loss final. When mourning is defined as a confrontation with the past that is supposed to lead to a closure of sorts, it seems very different from melancholy, grieving the traces of the past, or nostalgia, maintaining an intimate past while avoiding an unknown present. But perhaps all three are better understood as strategies in the circulation of traces to manifest an absence. An example would be the way in which Van Praag reinvented the ghetto by continuing the imaginary walks from his prewar oeuvre with Esther Ansell, a character in Zangwill's stories of life in the London East End. Once, 'you were so real because I only had to walk in the Lepelstraat to be surrounded by your brothers and sisters': the ambience of poor Jews, the trade, the busy gesticulation and diverse Yiddish accents. That vanished world could only be evoked by appealing to a literary character.[4] Similar feelings were felt by Hans Tiemeijer at the time he acted in the play:

> I confess once I was sitting . . . on a bench and saw what the Weesperstraat looked like and then I saw in my mind those shops that I knew from before, and aunt Saar, an old Jewish friend from the Lepelstraat. So yes, there I sat, crying.[5]

Shortly after the war, Jaap Meijer walked from the Rivierenbuurt, where he lived, to the city center to summon his own 'vanished ghetto,' going from door to door, naming the dead as an *ars memoriae*. Meijer was an historian and Anne's teacher at the Jewish Secondary. Otto gave him a copy of the diary: 'Anne had a slightly slow-sounding, piercing voice and remarkably warm, overly sensitive eyes. I can still clearly hear her somewhat German accent.' Meijer, like his pupil, had been deported to Belsen with his wife Liesje and toddler Ischa.[6] His essays actually were based on lectures held in a Belsen barracks. How could it have been that in the camp the incredible had happened: nostalgia for

> a world so crushingly poor, so devastatingly empty, so hopelessly disrupted. . . . We went through history for weeks. On paths too heavy with love and sorrow to stay upright. Staggering and stumbling through the Jewish wonder of Amsterdam – amid ruins and stone walls.[7]

For both wandering Jews, nostalgia was reflected in lavish portrayals of prewar life, capitalizing on a Jewry that had disappeared forever.

How did this work in the theater? Was there a similar deep desire to evoke the lost ghetto? And could the Anne Frank play meet this need? One likely candidate did not pass the vote, *Ghetto*, the successful fin-de-siècle play by Herman Heijermans. *Ghetto* (1899) was set in the Jewish quarter where a class struggle was unfolding, but also, according to the playwright, a culture clash between moderns, who moved out of religion, and traditionals, who would maintain a 'ghetto mentality.' Heijermans's assimilation play responded to current trends in Amsterdam where paupers encountered dramatic living conditions. Social risers first moved in the direction of the streets just beyond the quarter and then, if possible, to more distant neighborhoods. Not many were able to cross the river to where the Frank family came to live. All the same, mental distance grew. Jewishness became part of a culture of 'simultaneous discomfort and pleasure.'[8] Pleasure eventually translated into nostalgia coupled with a selective adherence to calendar and life cycle rituals. This is the nostalgia, reinforced by the camp experience, which Meijer identified in his self-diagnosis.

Heijermans's critique of ghetto life was pronounced, which is why Van Praag did not include 'the crudest and most shortsighted writer' in his anthology of ghetto literature.[9] According to Jaap Meijer *Ghetto*'s main character Sachel, whose name probably was a contraction of *sjacheren* (to chaffer) and Shylock, had all the traits of Shakespeare's character. This is the Ghetto Jew the respectable middle class liked to see, all the more so, as Meijer added acidly, 'who was already thinking of Auschwitz?' Despite or perhaps thanks to the clamor, Heijermans's script remained on the play list for decades only to disappear for a while after the war. In 1948, the Jewish Weekly referred to Heijermans's character as a Stürmer caricature.[10]

The prewar ghetto may have been unbearable to live and callously portrayed, it aroused a postwar longing all the same. Jewissance is the neologism that denotes the enjoyment one gets from entertaining oneself in 'acting Jewish' in an inordinate and transgressive manner.[11] Thus, instead of *Ghetto* there was *ghetto gein*, ghetto gaiety, which came in various forms like stand-up comedy and folk theater.

Jewissance as affect conjured up the surfaces of Jewish bodies. Max Tailleur was a *moppentapper*, a raconteur of jokes. His jokes certainly fell on fertile soil, but there was also disapproval of his caricatural shtick – in appearance and language. As a response to a drawn caricature for a book cover – made by Eppo Doeve, the designer of the Anne Frank program notes – the inevitable Stürmer equation came to the fore.[12] Jokes were his unique selling point but Tailleur also tried his hands on a number of revues and plays. He first joined the revitalized Rudolf Nelson Revue, followed by producing *Tewje the Milkman* in a version initiated by Willy Rosen. The stories of Sjolem Alejchem were already adapted for the stage. In 1935, Maurice Schwartz's Jüdisches Kunstlertheater had come over from New York to play an unforgettable Tewje. In 1942, Rosen worked on an operetta that led to a few dress rehearsals before he was deported to Westerbork – where he made theater – and to Auschwitz, where he was killed. The Dutch *Tewje* lived in 1920s Amsterdam, mixing 'some of the lost Eastern European

Jewish family life' with the Amsterdam 'vernacular' and 'quasi-Yiddish humor.' 'Finally something on the stage that we've missed for years,' that is, Jewish humor, as one of the postwar critics hailed the play.[13]

Every now and then postwar theater felt like one long citation from a chimeric prewar Jewish life. In 1951, Tailleur recreated the prewar ghetto atmosphere in *Dr Stieglitz*: 'a Jewish comedy by a Jewish ensemble.' This is a German play – 'so cleverly designed that the play can be applauded by philosemites and antisemites alike' – that was already performed with great success before the war.[14] Now it acquired new meaning. Although he recognized the clichés only too much, Jaap Meijer was at peace with it: everyone 'who even remembers the smallest bit of prewar Jewish life' had to laugh at this 'authentic Jewish Amsterdam theater.'[15] Here you could encounter the intensity, the vernacular, and the gesticulations that were as cliché as they were taken for the core of a Jewishness that was no longer there, from which people had distanced themselves but which was intimate all the same.

On February 18, 1951, the Maccabi club on Merwede Square organized the 'postwar premiere of the well-known comedy full of Yiddish humor,' *Potash and Perlmutter*. This was the theater against which the postwar dissemination policy was most literally established as when a city councilor pledged to bring sophisticated drama to people 'accustomed only to the cultural level of Potash and Perlmutter.'[16] But in fact, the show about two Jewish textile entrepreneurs was a resounding success with 600 performances in 1951–1953, followed by sequels with equal response. The show never seemed to go out of running. In the month of the premiere, one could visit the Anne Frank play and *Potash and Perlmutter* two days in a row in the same theater. Only 'bitter killjoys,' as one reviewer put it, would complain that after the persecution and the foundation of Israel, this farce, 'a complete anachronism of galut Jews,' should be left aside because of its tasteless portrayals of Jewishness.[17] It had been the great concern of the producer who was deeply attracted to the farce but feared audiences no longer would laugh at Jews 'after everything that had happened.'[18] But, as a matter of fact, they did and in big numbers. This was the kind of theater for which the Dutch employ the German verb *schmieren*: to play on effect – ham acting. But perhaps this was precisely what Van Praag longed for when he spoke of the 'busy gesticulation and the varied Yiddish accent' that had disappeared from the streets of Amsterdam.

Stock characters

Manifesting the persecution on stage was not limited to what became known as Holocaust Theater nor did traces from Jewish drama history only evoke nostalgic feelings. To the wise, many if not every show could contain references and some of these were more undesirable than ever. Postwar ruination – 'an active, ongoing process' of 'residues that abide and are revitalized' – refers to theatrical practices that seemed outdated yet persisted as unwelcome atavistic relics haunting the present. Among these relics that got stuck in repetition, a few Jewish stock characters – as comic foil or villain or both – had populated the theater world for centuries.[19] Shylock was clearly among these usual suspects. In the Netherlands, Shakespeare's *The Merchant of Venice* (1595) was mainly performed in corrupted adaptations since the Enlightenment. At the end of the nineteenth century, the hugely successful staging of the original script in a Dutch translation began. By then, the 'good Jew' also had made his appearance, with Lessing's *Nathan the Wise* (1783) as best, albeit much less staged, example.

In literature and drama, the Jewish type was featured by disposition and appearance. Jaap Meijer researched the appearance of Levie Zadok, a popular character created by a nineteenth-century hack writer who would also introduce Black Pete to the Netherlands, the black-faced servant of Sinterklaas (who would reach the secret annex via Miep in the shape of a *mombakkes* or mask). Various serial-like booklets and sketches full of 'Jewtalk' and songs on Levie Zadok appeared.[20] There were specific somatic markers, ways of talking, character traits and behavior that were thought to be recognizable 'Jewish.' Shylock had to look Jewish and the actor could make use of a make-up manual to learn how a 'Jewface' was to be realized. Until well after WWII, it was preferred that certain Jewish characters were played by 'real Jews' or to assume that Jewishness entails a certain authentic 'vivacity' in posture and gestures.

Long before the Shoah, objections were raised against the stereotyping – 'crooked-talking Jews' or 'overly Jewish rumpus' – on stage.[21] Individuals thus unsuccessfully protested against the alleged caricatures in *Ghetto*, *The Merchant of Venice* and *Potash and Perlmutter*.[22] Actor Cor Ruys had a lot of success with various Jewish types, including Potash in the 1930s.[23] *Sally Wegloper* was one of his characters whom the actor played on order and with some critical acclaim. Van Praag complimented the actor as one of the few non-Jews who could imitate an authentic Jew in language and gesture. 'For the Jewish-feeling Jew he managed to avoid the *risjes*' (i.e., everyday antisemitism). Nevertheless, the actor was called upon to stop his impersonation ('Cor, your *gein* really hurt me. . . . Sally Wegloper is not your *gabber*').[24] There was a thin line anyway between hyperbolic stage acting and the everyday talk of *smous* or *joodje* as *risjes*. In the run-up to the German occupation, when National Socialist hate speech already circulated in the Netherlands, the name Sally Wegloper developed into a code name for Jews in antisemitic literature and caricatures.

Prewar audiences could wallow in an excess of theatrical Jewishness in the numerous venues in the city center at a time when 'no mortal knew yet what the dissemination of culture was.' This was the domain of the real elite, the *Isra-elite*.[25] There were the assimilation plays in which Jewish family life was central, cabaret, farce and *variété*. From abroad, people got introduced to Yiddish theater, like the well-known play by S. Ansky, *The Dibbuk*. Little was left of the elaborate Jewish performing arts after the war. Postwar continental Europe had to reflect on its dramatic legacy after the physical and cultural genocide: about what to do with the archive of cliché characters, how to deal with the fraught past and how to reassess the collective memory of theater after the Shoah. Cor Ruys had already made his mind up: 'The days of Elias, Potash and Stieglitz are over' but, as he added, a Jew in a classic play like *The Merchant of Venice* still remains valid.[26]

When *The Merchant of Venice* was first performed in its original form, it became the prey of actor Louis Bouwmeester. Long after his death and well beyond WWII, every subsequent performance was measured by his portrayal of an old man in Oriental attire – copied after British actor Henry Irving – including a protruding beard. Although Shylock's postwar appearance and character were severely modified, the war continued to haunt the play. In 1952, the play was staged with mostly evasive remarks about its potentially problematic nature. In 1959, however, some critics began to raise serious objections. An example is a Jewish reviewer who called for the play to be annulled, revealing that in 1952 she felt uncomfortable but had allowed herself to be convinced by all kinds of artistic subtleties. Now staging this play was just 'insipid' and 'pure snobbery.'[27]

In 1959, Jules Croiset played the part of Lorenzo with father Max at his side as a brown-faced Prince of Morocco. Shortly after opening night, a letter arrived from The Hague Jewish Community, asking for an immediate cancellation. The board of the ensemble tried to dismantle the objections with a list of familiar counterarguments. None of these – the play wasn't antisemitic, many Jews liked the play – would convince the protesters. Most notable was the management's veiled threat that rather the mere exposure of Jews pleading for a ban would lead to antisemitism. The protesters explained that their objections needed to be understood in a post-Shoah world, one in which Jews found themselves in a precarious position and where it wasn't the script but the execution that mattered:

> Before 1940, staging 'The Merchant' was irrelevant for us. . . . We could ignore the objections which this or that Jewish spectator had against the play and perhaps against other plays with characters that are questionable from a Jewish point of view, because the peace and thus our position in the Netherlands seemed invulnerable.

The correspondence went back and forth a few more times and a meeting was set, but the affective distance was unbridgeable. The theater world aimed to restore the cultural order by reverting to prewar high culture, the correspondents saw a monster looming that perhaps once might have looked relatively harmless but since then had shown more than its teeth.[28] The monster was a pleasurable attraction for the troupe rather than a trauma that imposed itself or a danger that presented itself again and again, even although one authoritative voice, that of Abel Herzberg, firmly stated that the monster 'has lost almost all of its teeth.' One respected critic saw a painful meaningful match with the gruff post-Shoah atmosphere of returning Jews, when after the act in which Shylock was tried and convicted, the story happily continues in Act 5: 'No one in the audience was happy that Shylock was so grudgingly beaten, but no one longed for him back either.'[29]

Jewishness in the secret annex

When coining the Holocaust Jew, James E. Young referred to Anne's symbolic embodiment of the Shoah and postwar Jewishness. The stage in the Netherlands was diverse and the question arises how the Anne Frank play related to those other theatricalities. Clearly, the play did not satisfy the desire for Jewish ghetto nostalgia. Some of the old cliché's were there: Mr. Van Daan – sneaky selfish and well-fed – and Mrs. Van Daan – 'the Jewish mother' in her smothering and meddlesome character.' Still, there were no Yiddish folk types from the shtetl or the ghetto onstage. The play belonged in the Rivierenbuurt, not in the Jewish quarter. Anne as a stage character was the child of a Western, secular and assimilated family. The play's tone is more Hanukkah than Purim.

Jewish holidays are bound up with a ritualized look at the past. Besides the central moment of Pesach – and various *Haggadot* were written around Anne's diary – Purim fulfilled a distinctive role in the handling of the atrocities. Purim is the ritual of laughter, music and masquerades that is linked to the Book of Esther.[30] The heart of the Purim story is a genocide in the making. In fact, the Shoah could be construed as a Purim without Esther to save the day. In 1939, one Amsterdam Purim was celebrated with a recitation of Heijermans's *Ahasverus*.[31] After the war, in the German DP camps, Purim became a theatrical ritual of mock revenge and symbolic violence.[32] Postwar purims in Amsterdam were celebratory and elated, including acts by Max Tailleur and Wim Sonneveld, Yiddish theater, tombola, dance and children's festivities: 'Very enjoyable!' Yet often a recitation – quite a few times by Enny Mols – or a moment of commemoration was included. In 1948, a section of the Yiddish play *Nekomeh-nemer* ('Avengers') by Chaim Sloves was performed in Amsterdam. None of these ludic, joyful or retributive emotions have been associated with the Anne Frank play, the sentiment of which lay elsewhere.

Instead, *The Diary of Anne Frank* was about love, love for your fellow human beings, as Rob stated on national radio. There is a notable exchange here between Anne, Shylock and Nathan. The two archetypical Jews, Shylock and Nathan, nourished the postwar imaginations while taking on new meanings through the Shoah. Lessing's play was about the thoughtful Nathan who at the time of the Crusades proved himself as a model of tolerance. Because Nathan as a Jewish character differed so intensely from Shylock, a performance could be seen as an act of tolerance and civilization. In postwar Germany, this symbolic function was immediately understood. Whereas Shakespeare's play was banned early on after the war – in Frankfurt, in Berlin a theater opened its doors with the production of *Nathan*.[33] In 1954, the Viennese Burgtheater brought the play to the Netherlands. The message of tolerance was recognized, with respect to Germany. It has been argued that Lessing's play was the vehicle by which the postwar theater could address the Shoah before *The Diary of Anne Frank* brought this more directly to the stage. A production could be viewed as a return to civilization, repairing the rift that the war had struck.

The parallel between stage characters persisted. The Jewish actor Ernst Deutsch returned to Germany from exile to play the father figures of Nathan, Shylock and Otto in postwar theater. Remember how Spetter resisted the presentation of Otto the Wise onstage. There was talk of a nathanization of Shylock because the sharp edges of 'the Jew' had been filed away and empathy for his isolated position came to the fore – also in the Dutch 1959 production. Old Testament vengeance became New Testament forgiveness.

In the same way, there may have been a reincarnation of Nathan in Otto and Anne Frank with their tolerant and forgiving attitudes. Not a vengeful but a forgiving 'gentle' Jew. As such, the script's description of Otto Frank as a 'gentle, cultured European' is remarkable. Shakespeare employs the word gentle because of its potential for wordplay. Gentle is kind or meek and gentile is non-Jewish or Christian. So a gentle Jew is a contradiction in terms. The pun culminates in court when Shylock is urged not to insist on his right to retribution but instead to show compassion, Christian compassion that is: 'We all expect a gentle answer, Jew.' It was as if Anne gave the only morally correct answer to antisemitism and persecution, reproving Shylock and postwar survivors for sticking to their *ancient grudge*, their anger and resentment. The Venetian Jew should have responded along the lines of Otto's words: 'She puts me to shame.'

The play did contain various markers of a Jewish scenery, in any case, as portrayed in Jewish theater for the past half century: the centrality of the family, the reenactment of a ritual and the theme of exile and persecution.

Yet arguably all this could be shown to be nothing more than a bunch of signifiers with an empty center. The bigger the setup on the stage, the more the lack of Jewishness came to light. Some felt a 'non-Jewish atmosphere' or referred to actors as insufficiently Jewish. Where was that excess of Jewishness, that indefinable but 'typically and tragically Jewish essence in tone and manners . . . that is not connected to the events but to the people.'[34]

To anticipate the criticism, the Dutch production had come a long way in setting the play in a Jewish cultural memory of destruction. But not everyone was convinced. It was only after careful consideration that comedian and manager of the De la Mar, Wim Sonneveld, came to write Rob de Vries about the Dutch show. He had attended the New York performance and saw the play in Holland a few times. It was all very moving, but he was disappointed about what he only hesitantly came to call 'an incomprehensible negation': the absence of any palpable sense of Jewishness. There was a total lack of Jewish humor and 'the Hanukkah celebration was too Protestant and neat for my taste.'[35] Anne and Otto were thus insufficiently Jewish for some critics and spectators yet Jewish enough for the Nazis. Anne – on stage, for some in the diary as well – was lacking in true Jewishness and genuine piety. After the annexants discarded their imposed shibboleth upon arrival in the secret annex, they need to be nothing more than themselves – an impossibility in the given circumstances. Jewishness was imposed on the annexants, as symbolized in the force with which Peter rips off his yellow badge. Then what? In a diary conversation, Peter states that it would be easier if he could become a Christian after the war. Nobody would know about his credentials. He could even change his name. This was a known response to the persecution, but we remain in the dark as to how Peter van Pels actually would have proceeded. From the diary it seems Anne drew strength from a reinforced faith and an enhanced identification with Jews as a persecuted people. Perhaps the strength of her authorship lies precisely in Anne Frank's ability to assess and express the oppression exerted by the antisemitic stranglehold on her sense of Jewishness and Judaism. To say more about this, the diaries should be reread from the perspective of a non-essentialist Anne, writing, reading, contemplating, discussing and rewriting.

Presence and absence

There clearly are no final answers here, but instead new plays were staged to shed new light on old issues. In the year that the Eichmann trial was held, Max Frisch presented *Andorra*, a disturbing play about Jewishness as a stigma, whereas *The Wall* (adapted from John Hersey's book, 1950) celebrated Yiddishkeit amid the Warsaw Ghetto Uprising, a play that explicitly aimed to be a supplement to the Anne Frank play.[36] In that same year, De

Vries and Guttmann made their own contributions. Their ways had parted in 1956, in 1961 they each took their share of the play's legacy. Rob directed Bertolt Brecht's *The Resistible Rise of Arturo Ui*, a play that had been produced never before in the Netherlands and only recently in Germany. The satire, with Hitler disguised as a Chicago mob boss, was dear to him even though he expressed some anxiety because of the storyline that again came perilously close to his war experiences. The play was publicized in the same vein as the Anne Frank play: like a clarion call for young and old.

Karl Guttmann directed *The Tenth Man* (Paddy Chayefsky, 1959). The play drew on Ansky's *The Dibbuk* and was set in a New York synagogue. Critical response was on the whole supportive. Never before had so much Jewish faith been seen on the postwar stage: mysticism, liturgy, Kabbalah, dance. The play showed 'real Jewish' characters and actors, but critics also noticed the effort it took to evoke that true Jewishness: 'there were many pointed Yiddish remarks but few complete Yiddish men.' The script intended to be 'serious' but alternated this with *gein*. Nostalgia was key. Illustrative was the casting of one of the stars of the *Potash and Perlmutter* shows, and Sylvain Poons, an actor who put the Jewish *schlemiel* onstage for decades.[37]

For his part in Karl's play, Dick Scheffer won the Bouwmeester acting award, indeed named after the famous Shylock actor. Scheffer's parents, owners of a grocery store in the humblest part of the Jewish quarter, died in Auschwitz, he went into hiding as a 12-year-old. After the war, he changed his name from Isaäc Komkommer and struggled to become an actor. Why? 'We were not allowed to exist, we no longer existed administratively either. I had a great need to express myself, but I was not there.' Present yet absent. At drama school – with Willy Pos – Scheffer firmly declared he wanted to become a second Bouwmeester, 'doing Shylock': 'Doesn't a Jew have eyes? Doesn't a Jew have hands, bodily organs, a human shape, five senses, feelings, and passion.' The young student was advised to instead become the first 'Scheffer.' And that's what happened in *The Tenth Man*: 'I became myself . . . sixteen years after the war.'[38]

Notes

1 *De Maasbode*, May 4, 1957; *NIW*, May 10, 1957.
2 James E. Young, *Writing and rewriting the Holocaust: Narrative and the consequences of interpretation* (Bloomington, 1988), 109–113.
3 *Arnhemsche Courant*, December 12, 1955.
4 Siegfried E. van Praag, 'De Karavaanweg. Kroniek. Het land van Esther Ansell,' *NIW*, March 14, 1947; Siegfried E. van Praag, *Het Ghetto: Een beschouwing en bloemlezing van west- en oostjoodsche ghettoschetsen* (Zutphen, 1930); Ansell in J. Zangwill, *Kinderen van het Ghetto* (Amsterdam, 1896).

5 B&G: radio show *De stand van zaken*, December 2, 1983.
6 Evelien Gans, *Jaap en Ischa Meijer: Een joodse geschiedenis, 1912–1956* (Amsterdam, 2008).
7 Jaap Meijer, 'Het verdwenen ghetto,' 10 articles: *NIW*, September–October 1947–1948; Jaap Meijer, *Waar wij ballingen zijn. Essays over joodse letterkundigen* (Den Haag, 1967), 129–147.
8 Hans Goedkoop, *Geluk: Het leven van Herman Heijermans* (Amsterdam, 1996), 38; Selma Leydesdorff, *We lived with dignity: The Jewish proletariat of Amsterdam, 1900–1940* (Detroit, 1994).
9 Van Praag, *Het Ghetto*, 129.
10 *NIW*, September 3, 1948.
11 For jewissance, see: Nathan Abrams, *The new Jew in film: Exploring Jewishness and Judaism in contemporary cinema* (New Brunswick, 2012).
12 *NIW*, January 1, 1954.
13 Premiere, September 24, 1950. *Het Parool*, September 15, 1950; *De Telegraaf*, September 16, 1950; *NIW*, September 22, 29, 1950.
14 Johannes Andreas Löcker, *Armin Friedmann und das Unterhaltungstheater im Wien des beginnenden 20. Jahrhunderts* (Diplomarbeit Theater-, Film- und Medienwissenschaft, Universität Wien, 2014), 20.
15 Armin Friedmann und Ludwig Nerz, *Doktor Stieglitz. Familienkomödie [or: Lustspiel] in drei Akten* (Berlin and Vienna, December 19, 1919); Dutch postwar premiere, January 20, 1951; Meijer in *NIW*, January 26, 1951.
16 Albert de Roos in GA 0644, 8: 'Toneelspreiding kan werkelijkheid worden!' J.C. de Wit.
17 *Friese Koerier*, October 27, 1954.
18 Johan Kaart in *De Telegraaf*, January 15, 1953.
19 Ann Laura Stoler, 'Introduction,' in *Imperial debris: On ruins and ruination*, ed. Ann Laura Stoler (Durham, 2013), 1–35, 7; M.J.P.M. Weijtens, *Nathan en Shylock in de Lage Landen: De Jood in het werk van de Nederlandse letterkundigen uit de negentiende eeuw* (Groningen, 1971); Hans-Peter Bayerdorfer and Jens Matte Fischer, eds., *Judenrollen: Darstellungsformen im europäischen Theater von der Restauration bis zur Zwischenkriegszeit* (Tübingen, 2008).
20 As researched by Ewoud Sanders, *Lachen om Levie. Komisch bedoeld antisemitisme (1830–1930)* (Amsterdam, 2020); Ewoud Sanders, *Levi's eerste kerstfeest – Jeugdverhalen over jodenbekering 1792–2015* (Amsterdam, 2017).
21 *Het Vaderland*, June 19, 1915; *De Telegraaf*, June 20, 1915 (at the occasion of the first Dutch staging of *Potash and Perlmutter*).
22 At one performance of *Ghetto*, police had to remove protesters from the hall: *De Maasbode*, January 14, 1899.
23 *Moritz Marx*, a play by Rudolf Lothar and Hans Bachwitz; *Het Vaderland*, May 20, 1923; criticism in *Algemeen Handelsblad*, June 2, 1926; *Uncle Bernard* ('*Oom Bernard*') by Armin Friedmann and Hans Kattow. Premiere, October 21, 1922; review by Siegfried van Praag, *Centraal blad voor Israëlieten in Nederland*, February 16, 1923.
24 H. Kesnig, *Het Vaderland*, May 21, 1924; *De Vrijdagavond* 1, 35 (1924).
25 Meyer Sluyzer, *Er groeit gras in de Weesperstraat* (Amsterdam, 1962), 117–120.
26 *NIW*, September 26, 1952 (obit).
27 Jeanne van Schaik-Willing, 'Heine's Shylock en die van Paul Steenbergen,' *De Groene Amsterdammer*, January 10, 1959.

28 *Haags Gemeentearchief*, 0315-01 *De Haagse Kunststichting*, 597 Minutes of the board, February 27, May 26, 1959. Letter Nederlandsch-Israëlietische Gemeente 's Gravenhage, secretaris A. Emanuel, to Cees Laseur, May 10, 1959, includes appendix with letter Nederlandsch Israëlietische Gemeente te's Gravenhage to the *Haagse Kunstkring*, May 8, 1959. For an early protest: *NIW*, March 13, 1925.

29 Herzberg in *Algemeen Handelsblad*, January 29, 1959; Shylock as monster: Anton Koolhaas in *Vrij Nederland*, February 7, 1959. Heinrich Heine's portrayal of Shylock as a 'wehr-wolf, a hated fabulous being who yearns for blood' was known to critics.

30 It has been argued that the biblical text itself is a comedy: The JPS Bible Commentary, *Esther: The traditional Hebrew text with the new JPS translation*, commentary by Adele Berlin (Philadelphia, 2003); Anne Frank and Pesach: Liora Gubkin, *You shall tell your children: Holocaust memory in American passover ritual* (New Brunswick, 2007), 96–123.

31 *NIW*, February 28, 1964.

32 Zeev W. Mankowitz, *Life between memory and hope: The survivors of the Holocaust in occupied Germany* (Cambridge, 2002), 196.

33 *NIW*, January 3, 1946; *Trouw*, August 20, 1945.

34 *Het Parool*, October 2, 1956. This latter remark was based on the German productions.

35 UvA: Brsonn014, Sonneveld to De Vries, May 20, 1957.

36 Max Frisch, *Andorra: Stück in zwölf Bilder*n (Frankfurt, 1961), staged in the Netherlands; Millard Lampell, *The wall: A play in two acts* (New York, 1961). A Dutch ensemble took an option on the play, but this did not lead to a production.

37 *Nieuwe Haarlemse Courant*, November 6, 1961; UvA: Interview Sylvain Poons by Fred Florusse, May 14, 1975.

38 Premiere, September 23, 1961, Tilburg, *Algemeen Handelsbad*, *Nieuwe Tilburgsche Courant*, September 25, 1961; *Algemeen Dagblad*, September 26, 1961; Guttmann in *NIW*, April 21, 1972; Scheffer, *Het Parool*, November 11, 1977.

Figure 12 Anne and Peter in Scene 2: 'What are you doing?' 'Taking it off.' 'But you can't do that. They'll arrest you if you go out without your star.' 'Who's going out?' (Maria Austria/MAI)

Conclusions

After events and affects

[A] gift from Anne.

–Jacqueline van Maarsen, Anne's best friend

From milieu de mémoire to lieu de mémoire

The Diary of Anne Frank is one of the critical plays to understand how postwar theater picked up on the genocidal past. Much has been written about the play already, but in many instances this covers the script, leaving the stage history underexposed. This monograph was intended to make up for this shortfall and thus provide a better understanding of the impact of theater in surfacing the Shoah: on the audience, the critics, the cast and even on those who stayed at home. As I flipped through the sources, I was deeply impressed by the life histories of the two protagonists, Rob de Vries and Karl Guttmann, the effort they put it and the commotion their joint venture caused. The lively conversations with the two cast members brought the performances even closer. As a historian I have tried to convey all this in an account of the stage production as a dramatic momentum in Dutch and European postwar history.

I began with the observation that theater could never provide an unmediated representation of 'the Holocaust' or 'the diary.' Neither the words nor the theatrical forms to manifest the remains and memories of the past were readily available. Searching for words and inspired by Assmann's metaphors of memory, I came to think in terms of Walter Benjamin's excavation and flash and Jacques Derrida's traces and specters to investigate 'the ongoing, uneven, and destabilizing intrusion of irrevocable pasts into an unredeemed present.'[1] This endeavor involved finding a balance between the exclusive and spectacular momentum of the theatrical performance on the one hand and its repetition on the other, harking back to the past of war and drama and echoing into the future.

DOI: 10.4324/9781032034324-7

Research consisted of examining how words, artifacts and locations were recognized as traces of a past that had yet to take its public form, and then how these sites and citations became part of a circulation of signs to express relationships of likeness and identification. Empathy as affect can be understood as a process of recognizing traces of identity and difference, an interpretation that parallels Dominique LaCapra's concept of empathic unsettlement, a stance situated between disengagement and 'full identification with, and appropriation of, the experience of the other.'[2] It is in this way that Anne Frank as a sign became a mark *to part*, in both senses of the verb:[3] it bound those who felt addressed as empathic subjects, but alienated those who disapproved or felt subjected – in part because of the diary's supposed ethical appeal, as manifested in the repetitive citation of the well-known aphorism.

The play impacted 1950s Dutch society's handling of the murder of more than 100,000 Jewish civilians and played a key role in a process that stretched far beyond the shores of the theatrical field. The staging was an event that sparked a proliferation of performative acts to engage with the memory of the Shoah. Like a flywheel, it put affective signs into circulation, dating, localizing and articulating the atrocities and naming the unnameable – without an umbrella term being available – and thus allowing them to enter the field of communication and convention while addressing – or interpellating – people.

One of the most recent of these acts took place on September 23, 2020, when 91-year-old Jacqueline van Maarsen, Anne's friend Jopie, laid the foundation stone for the National Holocaust Monument. Mrs. Van Maarsen was invited because of a donation after auctioning a handwritten page by Anne from her sister's *poesiealbum* – an album amicorum for children, but the bond with Anne was as important. When asked, Van Maarsen explained she considered the donation to be 'a gift from Anne.'[4] The ritual connected the memorial with one of the last persons to have known Anne Frank. Anne's milieu de mémoire was symbolically inscribed onto a belated site of memory. This was the result of a long process. The alignment of Anne, her writing and various sites and symbols went full steam ahead with the play but began earlier when the gift is seen as one step in a circulation that includes the gift of the diary on Anne's 13th birthday, the rhyme in the poesiealbum and the transfer of the diary from Miep to Otto. The attachment of affect, commonly associated with a gift-exchange, had imbued the artifacts with the spirit of its first owner.[5]

It was Jeroen Krabbé, the director of the second production, who gave Van Maarsen the idea of donating the proceeds of the auction to the memorial. Krabbé was a member of the recommendation committee for the memorial, just as Rob de Vries had been with regard to the memorialization of Anne – for instance, in renaming the Montessori school after Anne Frank on the day she would have turned 28 (June 12, 1957). Rob and Otto had been discussing the possibilities of doing so after the city council thought of naming a street after Anne, which was to be announced at the play's premiere.[6] Similar activities were discussed in Frankfurt, Anne's place of birth.[7] May 3, a day before the play's special performance, the *Anne Frank Stichting* was founded to renovate the structure and develop peace work in the spirit of Anne. The play was not a magic wand though. The next day, May 4, when the play was staged in the municipal theater, no Shoah victims were officially commemorated. The memorial was focused on an undivided nation in which the heroes of the resistance occupied a prominent place. Shoah victims were marked in the protocol from 1966 onward.

'Holocaust Jews'

Once upon a time there was a performance of *The Diary of Anne Frank* that was so flawed that when the Nazis pounded on the door, the audience began to roar: 'they're behind the bookcase!' This is a well-known joke by Dutch comedian Freek de Jonge. In fact, it is one that was already made by the Hacketts privately in 1957 after being informed of the French production that made the characters 'so unpleasant and disagreeable that an audience would welcome the Gestapo taking them.'[8] Making the joke public on stage – the comedian would later clarify he only cited from what was available in the public domain – is part of the changing sensibilities from the 1980s.

At the time of the second professional production, the play and the deployment of Anne's persona were seen more than ever as a screen memory, a way of concealing rather than revealing the latent effect of the past in the present. New theater, a new clarion call, was needed to recalibrate the theatrical engagement with the Shoah, resulting in challenging new theater. Skloot's selection in his *The Theatre of the Holocaust* holds a number of plays – by Charlotte Delbo and George Tabori among others – that follow an entirely different treatment of the persecution.[9]

James E. Young's argument regarding the emergence of Anne Frank as the 'Holocaust Jew' suggests that the figure of Anne became a shibboleth not only for empathy but also for passing the test of Jewishness. Young pointed out how some Jews felt uncomfortable with this and because of this went in search of alternative literary and theatrical forms. There was also skepticism and aversion in the Netherlands, in the 1950s and again in the 1980s. Actual commotion, however, arose around another play, a new watershed event for a new generation.

In 1987, student director Johan Doesburg undertook an attempt to stage Rainer Werner Fassbinder's *Garbage, The City and Death.*[10] Dating back to the late 1970s, protests had so far made a German staging impossible. The Dutch production was to be Doesburg's graduation project for drama school. Main character in Fassbinder's play was a nameless Rich Jew, a ruthless entrepreneur who, as critics claimed, was equipped with every possible antisemitic stereotype pertaining to money, sex and violence. Ischa Meijer – who as a toddler was incarcerated in Belsen and was professionally active as a writer and an actor – initially signed for the main part. When the premiere auditorium backed out a Jewish interest group got wind of the project and called for the play to be cancelled.[11] To top it all off, one of the protesters, Jules Croiset, was kidnapped for antisemitic reasons while a few 'famous Jews' found threatening letters in their mailbox. It soon turned out to be a painful self-abduction, which led, as Croiset would put it, to a second 'storm of emotions that [this time] I had unleashed myself.'[12] Years later, Doesburg would produce the play without any problems, and, after another two decades, he would direct his own take on the diary: *Achter Het Huis* ('Behind the House').[13]

The Fassbinder affair gave rise to a rich cultural production. Ischa Meijer wrote a play and Harry Mulisch came up with a short novel that gave an alternative perspective on Croiset's motivations. Comedian Freek de Jonge (whose family was one of the recipients of the threatening letters) responded angrily with a show in which he pre-announced to burn Mulisch's book on national television.[14]

There was significant input from Jews who were young in the war or had grown up after: people who would not suffer from alleged antisemitism in silence as they ostentatiously made clear. Of course, that did not imply all supported a ban, far from it, but for many their Jewish identity, linked to antisemitism and the Shoah, came to play a major role in their life. Croiset is a case in point. In 1956, he was ignorant about nor interested in things Jewish. At least, of what he later came to appreciate as Jewish and for which he took a number of study courses.[15] He was not alone in this. But the Shoah didn't land in the same way everywhere. Meijer's attitude was one of ironic reflection regarding the feelings of 'first-' and 'second-generation' Jews and the weight of the past. This was the kind of discussion with which he was familiar, but which certainly did not relate to his own family. Father Jaap Meijer may have written nostalgic pieces after the war, but at home he remained completely silent about 'the camp.'

The Fassbinder uproar was a milestone, if only because after a century of complaints, a 'Jewish lobby' had finally succeeded in putting a stop to a disturbing play. Fassbinder had attempted to loosen up a fossilized cultural memory, to make present what had become willfully obscured: ongoing unease with the presence of Jews and the limits of public shows of empathy. What if not Anne spoke to us from the air to bring us her message of love, but Shylock? What if 'the Jew' didn't gently look forward to a bright future like Otto Frank, but instead put things in order, standing tall for retaliation surfing a public wave of guilt and private waves of hatred? Fassbinder wrote an alternative script for Shylock and Anne, retracing what had been erased, but the protesters didn't want these traces to surface. Ischa had another urgent question. How to be or behave like a Jew, if not like Anne Frank or the Shylock-esque Rich Jew? How to be or become an 'authentic Jew' at the end of the twentieth century? Perhaps, Ischa thought aloud, the clue is located in Croiset's fake abduction: 'So this is how you *act* at being a Jew.'[16] He had set the example himself with his German one-man show *Der Sympathische Jude*.[17]

Remembering Anne Frank theater

Anne Frank gained a lasting symbolic presence in the theater world. When the first production ended, a small semi-professional company seized the opportunity to give shape to the ideal of cultural dissemination even more by traveling with a small set along a string of minor venues: Etten, Dordrecht, Mill, Ede, Vierlingsbeek, Zundert, Uden, Rozenburg: 'The true dissemination of theater, without a penny subsidy.'[18] Krabbé's initiative (1984–1985) led to the second professional production, followed by a third in 1995.[19]

In 1986, the critical edition of the diary was published. Harry Mulisch was invited to speak at the presentation, so that he finally felt obliged to read the diary! After another decade, dramatist Wendy Kesselman was commissioned to 'newly adapt' the Hacketts script, including insights from the critical edition. The play premiered in 1997 in New York. At some point after the turn of the century, this script was presented to Rob's son, Edwin de Vries, with the proposal to produce a show and take on the part of Otto. That would have been something but De Vries judged the script dated and suggested to write an entirely new one. However, the writers Jessica Durlacher and Leon de Winter were ahead of him. They would script *Anne* that premiered in 2016, soon followed by the aforementioned *Behind the House*. Both scripts clearly reference the Hacketts script. Even without these new adaptations, the Hacketts script left its mark on a Theater of the Holocaust. Anne Frank is very much present in volume 2 of Skloot's collection of Holocaust plays, with references in three of the six plays. Citations remain in abundance as befits the performing arts. At the time of the proofs for this monograph, the second part of a much-viewed 'video diary' by the Anne Frank House has been uploaded to YouTube, while a trailer announces a feature film about the friendship between Hanneli and Anne to appear next month. Undoubtedly there is more to come. More generally, since 2010 the Dutch *Theater na de Dam Foundation* has been organizing performances on May 4 to revive interest in the commemoration: 'a custom that began in the 1960s for reading appropriate theater texts to the public after Remembrance Day is once again taken up and continued in a larger way.' It's fitting to add the unsuccessful 1957 initiative to perform *The Diary of Anne Frank* each year on May 4 to this genealogy.

I end where this monograph started, referencing the life histories of Karl Guttmann and Rob de Vries. In 2016, Edwin de Vries and his son Sam performed a dramatized version of Rob's stunt in Westerbork, *Westerbork Serenade*, in the National Holocaust Museum (in formation). The play not only was a tribute to father and grandfather Rob. The title references a song sung and recorded by the comedians Johnny & Jones (Nol van Wesel and Max Kannewasser, Bergen-Belsen 1945) while in Westerbork. 'Jopie' saw them perform in Amsterdam just after Anne went into hiding.

Karl Guttmann, who died in 1995, returned to Bielitz at late age for a reunion and a documentary about the gymnasium, and a theater production with a local Polish ensemble. He once more returned for a memorial service for the destruction of the synagogue that was organized on his initiative by a local historian. He was to recite Psalm 44, 'an uncompromising psalm,' in which after the destruction, the recitator accuses God and begs him to assert his authority. I couldn't help but be reminded of his Bialik recitation as a young student: '*Awake! Why do You sleep, O Lord? Arise! Do not cast us off forever*.'[20]

Notes

1 Michael Rothberg, *The implicated subject: Beyond victims and perpetrators* (Stanford, 2019), 9. Intermediary text – and Derrida reference – is Berber Bevernage, *History, memory, and state-sponsored violence* (New York, 2012).
2 Dominique LaCapra, 'Trauma, absence, loss,' *Critical Inquiry* 25, 4 (1999): 696–727.
3 Jacques Derrida, *Sjibbolet: Voor Paul Celan* (Nijmegen, 2015).
4 NPO TV Show *Tijd voor Max*, January 25, 2018.
5 Gift-exchange is a recurring feature in the relationship between Van Maarsen, Anne and Otto Frank. Jacqueline van Maarsen, *Anne en Jopie. Leven met Anne Frank* (Amsterdam, 1990).
6 GA 0644, 183: Frank to De Vries, November 8, 1956.
7 *Frankfurter Allgemeine*, March 2, 1957.
8 David L. Goodrich, *The real Nick and Nora: Frances Goodrich and Albert Hackett, writers of stage and screen classics* (Carbondale, IL, 2004), 236.
9 Robert Skloot, ed., *The theatre of the Holocaust*, vol. 2 (Madison, 1982, 1999).
10 On the affair, see: Evelien Gans, *Gojse nijd & joods narcisme: Over de verhouding van joden en niet-joden in Nederland* (Amsterdam, 1992).
11 Interview Ensel – Johan Doesburg, October 21, 2020.

12 UvA: Jules Croiset 200000, 493.039, Croiset to Mr. Tinholt, Chair of the Association of Theater Halls ('Letter of Excuse'), January 12, 1988.
13 Premiere November 11, 2017; Ilja Leonard Pfeijffer, *Achter het huis* (Alkmaar and Amsterdam, 2018).
14 Ischa Meijer, *Ons dorp, de schoonheid en het leven*. Premiere, September 9, 1988; Harry Mulisch, *Het theater, de brief en de waarheid* (Amsterdam, 2000); Freek de Jonge, *De conferencier, het boekenweekgeschenk en de leugen*. Premiere, March 14, 2000.
15 Interview Ensel – Croiset, August 8, 2020.
16 Ischa Meijer, 'Hoe speel je een Jood,' in *Ik heb niks tegen antisemieten: Ik lééf ervan*, ed. Roni Palach (Amsterdam, 2020), 179–183.
17 Ischa Meijer, *Izzi M. Der Sympathische Jude* (Berlin, 1983).
18 *De Schouwspelers*, direction: Coba Kelling, premiere, November 12, 1960; *De Linie*, January 28, 1961.
19 Direction: Arda Brokmann, premiere, January 21, 1995.
20 *NIW*, May 22, 1992.

Index